OPPORTUNITIES

in

6-15-04 AH

Gerontology and Aging Services Careers

OPPORTUNITIES

in

Gerontology and Aging Services Careers

REVISED EDITION

DISCARD

ELLEN WILLIAMS

VGM Career Books

Chicago   New York   San Francisco   Lisbon   London   Madrid   Mexico City
Milan   New Delhi   San Juan   Seoul   Singapore   Sydney   Toronto

Library of Congress Cataloging-in-Publication Data

Williams, Ellen, 1951–
    Opportunities in gerontology and aging services careers / Ellen Williams.
    —Rev. ed.
        p.   cm.—(VGM opportunities series)
    Includes bibliographical references.
        ISBN 0-07-139045-6 (paperback)
        1. Gerontology—Vocational guidance—United States.   2. Aged—
    Services for—United States   I. Title.   II. Series.

    HQ1064.U5 W59218   2003
    305.26'023'73—dc21   2002066390

1 2 3 4 5 6 7 8 9 0   LBM/LBM   1 0 9 8 7 6 5 4 3 2

ISBN 0-07-139045-6

McGraw-Hill books are available at special quantity discounts to use as premiums and
sales promotions, or for use in corporate training programs. For more information,
please write to the Director of Special Sales, Professional Publishing, McGraw-Hill, Two
Penn Plaza, New York, NY 10121-2298. Or contact your local bookstore.

This book is printed on acid-free paper.

I dedicate this book to my parents, Mr. and Mrs. Earl Williams, and my grandparents, Mr. and Mrs. James Carr and Mr. and Mrs. Edward Williams. By the examples of how they lived their lives, they taught me what it means to age with strength and humor, love and faith. And that is the best gerontology lesson anyone can teach.

Contents

Foreword

Simone de Beauvoir has written in *The Coming of Age* that the issues of age challenge the whole society and put the whole society to the test.

Ellen Williams has accepted the challenge and written a timely and useful book about the burgeoning field of gerontology. She presents a comprehensive overview of career opportunities arising out of the presence and the needs of the growing numbers of old people in the United States and around the world.

Williams indicates the collaboration of many disciplines and bodies of knowledge required both to work with old people and to dispel the myths and misconceptions about late life held in our competitive society. She also stresses the need for personal understanding of old people and identification with them in growing old. She recognizes the differences among old people in education, income, social class, ethnic and racial origin, and she affirms the goal of "quality of life" and involvement in community affairs for all older Americans. I especially welcome Williams's emphasis on programs that bring the old and the young together.

I write this foreword from personal experience. I am one of those long-lived survivors. At eighty-nine I consider old age not a "problem" or a social disaster, but a challenge and a triumph of public health and the capacity of human beings to deal with social and technological change. After I turned sixty-five, I maintained for twenty years a demanding and exhilarating schedule of lecturing at universities, appearing on TV and radio, and writing. The Gray Panthers has successfully brought people of different ages together—young people, old people, middle-aged people—to work for social justice and change and share the universal experience of growing up and growing old.

Mandatory retirement is a social waste and should be eliminated. Reforms are urgently needed in the workplace to enable and encourage older workers to continue working. Gray Panthers recommend such innovations as part-time employment, work teams of older and younger workers, sabbatical leaves, and job sharing.

This is a new age. Read *Opportunities in Gerontology and Aging Services Careers* and go for the challenge ahead!

Margaret (Maggie) E. Kuhn
Founder and National Convener
The Gray Panthers
Philadelphia, Pennsylvania

Preface

THE NEED FOR this text, *Opportunities in Gerontology and Aging Services Careers*, is well supported by the ever-rising number of older adults, a population that by this very growth will need a labor force greater in number and diversity to meet its many needs. These personnel demands will be met by a cross section of many fields such as communications, health services, social work, nutrition, consumer affairs, recreation, housing, and many others that will be explored in this text. Research has indicated that there will be severe gaps in services to older adults unless gerontology training programs and careers quickly move to catch up with the population growth.

Statistics clearly illustrate that older adults are a major segment of our society. This large percentage of older adults is attributed to low birth rates and extended life spans due to better lifestyle habits, improved health care, life-extending medical technology, and an overall higher standard of living. As of 2000, there were 34.7 million Americans over age 65, or 12.7 percent of the population. In 1996, the first baby boomers turned 50, becoming the largest aging cohort in our nation's history; by 2011, 77 million baby boomers will turn 65. In 1900, in America, the average life span was 49; now, one hundred years later, that life span has been extended to 79 years for women and 74 years for men. In 1900, about one in twenty-five Americans was over 65; today one in eight is over 65. The U.S. Census Bureau has predicted that the over-65 population will grow two to two-and-a-half times over the next forty years to more than seventy million people, and that the population of those over 85 will triple to nine million. The elderly population is expected to more than double by the year 2050; by 2030, as many as one in five people could be 65 or older. People who survive to age 65 can expect to live an average of nearly eighteen more years. People over 85 are the second fastest growing segment of the older adult population. By 2050, seniors 85 and older are expected to comprise 5 percent of the U.S. population. There are 36,000 centenarians now in America; it is estimated that this number will rise to 266,000 by 2020. Centenarians are the fastest growing segment of the population. Due to this increasing life expectancy, future population reports will now need to distinguish between ages 85 and 94, and ages 95 and older, separately.

Gerontology must be viewed from the perspective of global aging. Around the world, older adults face many of the same difficulties such as unemployment, rising health care costs, inadequate housing, and dwindling caregiver resources. Older adults are becoming an increasing majority, not only throughout our nation, but also throughout our world. According to United Nations projections, 828 million people will attain the age of 65 or above in 2025. Most of these people will reside in developing regions, with the majority in Asia. Worldwide, nations are joining together to address the global issues impacting the elderly. The 5th European Congress of Gerontology will be held July 2003 in Spain. The 7th International Federation on Aging Global Conference will be held in Singapore in 2004, the 8th in Denmark in 2006. In June 2005, Brazil will host the 18th World Congress of International Association of Gerontology.

It is customary to cite the growth of the elder population as justification for increased interest in gerontology careers; however, it should be noted that the rationale for this book goes far beyond demographics. Professionally trained gerontology personnel are needed not only because there is an increased number of older adults but also because there must be assurance that this expanded life span is accompanied by an expanded quality of life. To put it another way, what is the point of living longer if the quality of that prolonged life is unacceptable, if not in some cases intolerable? This book is guided by the belief that the assurance of a life of good quality for older adults is not an option in this world but a moral imperative.

ACKNOWLEDGMENTS

I AM PLEASED to acknowledge the following sources of resource information: Joy C. Lobenstine, Association for Gerontology in Higher Education; Bruce Craig, Aging Training Program Specialist, Administration on Aging; Ann Kahl, Bureau of Labor Statistics; Ellen Sullivan, Lansing Community College; Erma Tetzloff, Administration on Aging; Jeanne Miller, Research Librarian, Institute of Gerontology, University of Michigan; Theresa Lambert, Director of Development, National Association of State Units on Aging; Lois Stewart, the New Jersey Division on Aging; Legan Wong, Program Specialist, Region II, Administration on Aging; Richard Connelly, School of Nursing, University of Utah Gerontology Center; Mimi Paperman, Director of RSVP, Senior Services, Essex County, New Jersey; Jane Shulman, Allyn & Bacon Publishers; and the National Council on Aging Public Relations Department.

The following resources are acknowledged: 2000–2001 *Occupational Outlook Handbook*; National Aging Information Center of the Administration on Aging; *A Profile of Older Americans: 2001* by the Administration on Aging and the U.S. Department of Health and Human Services; U.S. Bureau of the Census, National Center of Health Statistics, Bureau of Labor Statistics; Interagency Forum on Aging-Related Statistics; University of Rhode Island Gerontology Program; Alliance for Retired Americans; Gerontological Society of America; Alabama Gerontological Society; Alliance Continuing Care Network; Association for Gerontology in Higher Education; New York State Office on Aging; University of North Texas Applied Gerontology Department.

Tom Toale, Mary Cosgrove, and William D. Russiello, Esq., are acknowledged for their contributions. Special acknowledgment is extended to my supportive family and, in particular, my mother, who assisted in compiling the appendixes and has always encouraged my dreams.

1

Exploring a Career in Gerontology

We are daily reminded through our news and media that the older population is becoming an increasing majority of our worldwide population. This has led many to consider careers serving this growing clientele. The field of gerontology incorporates a wide variety of professions. The individual determines what profession he or she wishes to pursue in order to work with and for older adults. Gerontology is a multidisciplinary field; in career preparation, aging is not studied in isolation, but in conjunction with a professional area such as law, social work, business, or architecture.

Defining Gerontology and Geriatrics

"Gerontology" is the study of the aging process; it encompasses the physical, emotional, legal, intellectual, economic, social, environmental, and psychological dynamics of that process. It is also the study of the impact of the aging population on society. Further, this knowledge is applied to program planning and policy making, for example, related to housing, employment, and medical care. A career in gerontology is a career that serves one or more of those aspects of the aging process, aging in society, and service delivery to older adults. Those engaged in any of these many possible gerontology careers are referred to as "gerontologists." Throughout this book you will be exposed to the vast number of career possibilities in gerontology.

The older population is highly diverse in all aspects, including, for example, economics, ethnicity, race, gender, education, and health; career options in gerontology are as diverse as the population. Gerontologists work in administration, policy planning, advocacy, social services, research, and education. They work with both frail and well elderly and in a variety of settings. They also work with those who are in some way responsible for the welfare of older adults, such as their employers, caregivers, or service providers.

Unfortunately, many job seekers do not associate careers in gerontology with the vast number of opportunities available. For instance, they are not aware of such job titles as elder law attorney or senior employment counselor, geriatric care manager or geropsychologist. This lack of awareness is largely due to the public's widespread misinformation on the characteristics of the older adult population itself. For instance, many still wrongly believe that a large number of older adults live in nursing homes. This is untrue. At any one time, only 5 percent are institutionalized. Despite this fact, the general public still associates aging with ill health and dependency, leading them to believe that gerontology careers are confined solely to health careers in nursing homes and hospitals.

This narrow view leads professionals to avoid exploration of gerontology as a possible field. In its new emergence as a multidisciplinary field, gerontology is a profession receptive to committed individuals interested in creating positions that match their skills to the needs of the elderly. It is a major aim of this book to dispel those false stereotypes about aging that deter individuals from entering the gerontology field.

Because gerontology has, unfortunately, been "biomedicalized," that is, defined along a health care model, many current professionals working with and for older adults in a variety of nonmedical capacities do not even realize that they are, in actuality, gerontologists in gerontology careers! Because there has been the widely accepted misconception that all older adults are in some way needy and dependent on rehabilitative services, the medical model of gerontology has overshadowed any other thinking. People do not fully understand the growth of the gerontology field because they do not fully appreciate how many careers are gerontology careers. Because a career is listed as, for instance, social worker or financial counselor with no mention of the word "gerontology," it is not surprising that the public does not associate these fields with gerontology or aging services. For example, then, a human resources director responsible for retirement planning programs and eldercare services would undoubtedly not realize that he or she actually had the job title of industrial gerontologist.

It should be noted that "gerontology" and "geriatrics" are not synonymous. Gerontology refers to the sociocultural influences on aging and the relationship of older adults to society. Gerontology careers are those that facilitate satisfying interrelationships between older adults and the social and environmental worlds in which they live. A retirement counselor, for example, is a gerontologist because he or she is involved in assisting the employee in making choices conducive to a satisfying retirement lifestyle. A social worker training elders to be peer counselors in their own bereavement support group would also be a gerontologist. These are just two examples of the many gerontology careers one may pursue.

"Geriatrics," on the other hand, refers to the medical areas of gerontology. It is concerned with the health and wellness needs of older adults and their caregivers. This encompasses a broad spectrum of health care. For instance, a geriatric dentist is one who specializes in the oral health of older adults. The term "geriatric" before an occupation indicates that the occupation involves a medical service to older adults. For example, a geriatric consultant might provide technical assistance to designers of assisted living communities. Similarly, a person working "in geriatrics" is one employed in some area of medical service, such as a community mental health center serving elderly clients. The word "geriatrician" describes a physician whose patients are older adults. Researchers are in demand in the geriatric field to address such issues as genetic engineering and Alzheimer's disease. "Gerontology" or "gerontologist" are generally used as the umbrella terms for geriatric and nongeriatric positions; however, it is preferable to use the terms "geriatrics" and "geriatrician" if the job is in a health care field. Gerontology and geriatric professions involve either direct service or indirect service to older adults. Direct service positions involve direct interaction with elders and/or their caregivers, as in the work of a lawyer or nurse's aide. Indirect service positions involve working on behalf of elders and/or their caregivers without direct contact with them, for instance, as a scientist researching Alzheimer's disease or as a legislative aide on the Senate Special Committee on Aging.

Which Gerontology Career Is for Me?

In preparing for a gerontology career, the individual needs to adopt a creative, proactive approach. This individual must first start from an awareness of the type of gerontology career he or she wishes to pursue.

The following self-inventory should be taken:

- Why am I interested in pursuing a career in gerontology?
    - —have a strong intrinsic interest in the field
    - —enjoy working with older adults
    - —understand that this is a growing field due to the burgeoning of the older adult population
    - —would like to translate my volunteer work to employment in gerontology
    - —have been told that I have an innate ability to work with older adults
    - —will help me understand my own aging process
    - —was advised by colleagues, friends, and/or family
    - —has been a long-standing interest of mine that I am just now following through on
    - —see this as career advancement
    - —expands my employability and marketability
    - —complements my work background and skills
    - —will provide more income
    - —bored with present job
    - —other
- Why am I interested in gerontology?
- What type of work do I currently enjoy doing or want to learn how to do? How could this work be applied in a geron-

tology career? (Example: If I enjoy conducting recreational activities, would I consider working as a recreation director in a retirement community or a long-term-care facility? If I identify myself as a writer, would I want to be a reporter for a publication on senior lifestyles in the new millennium?)

- What are my strongest work skills? What jobs have I enjoyed the most and why?
- What are the major strengths I bring to the job search? Major weaknesses?
- Did some personal experiences with an older adult(s) inspire me to consider gerontology as a career? Explain.
- Did some professional experience(s) lead me to become interested in gerontology as a career? Explain.
- What excites me about the prospects of a career in gerontology? What concerns me?
- Do I prefer to work in administration, direct service, research, education, or policy making? Do I want to have direct contact with older adults, or will I work on their behalf without direct contact?
- Do I have a preference for working with the frail or well elderly?
- Do I want to work with individual older adults or with groups? Do I want to work with their caregivers, employers, or service providers?
- What type of setting do I wish to work in? (For example, life care community, government office, senior citizens center, adult day care, educational institution.)
- Do I prefer to work with the same clients and/or in the same setting over an extended period of time, or would I prefer a variety of clients and settings?

- Do I want to be employed by an agency, or do I want to be self-employed?

Responses to this self-assessment provide a valuable basis for reflection on one's gerontology career interests. The remainder of this text will explore the scope of gerontology career options as well as the training and job-seeking skills necessary to obtain these careers.

Theories of Aging

One of the most counterproductive stereotypes affecting delivery of services to the elderly has been the disengagement theory. The *individual disengagement* theory proposes that as individuals age, physical and mental limitations cause them to willingly disengage from their former roles, such as those of mother or community volunteer. The *social disengagement* theory states that society withdraw its role expectations from the elderly at the same time that they individually disengage. This false reasoning caused a reduction in programs for older adults based on the assumption that older adults were "too tired and resigned to bother." This rationale also led to limited expansion of careers in gerontology. For example, the view was why should a senior volunteer coordinator be hired when the disengagement theory recommended curtailing efforts to actively involve the elderly?

This theory has since been successfully challenged by more popular and healthier views, i.e., the continuity and activity theories. The continuity theory states that the older adult is not radically different from what he or she was throughout life; that personality and interests remain fairly consistent through these later years. The continuity theory successfully rejects the notion that one suddenly becomes a different person merely upon arriving at a certain birthday. The activity theory states that while some roles may be eliminated in the later years—such as worker or spouse—new roles can be adapted to maintain one's self-esteem. Reinforced by these positive views in the continuity and activity theories, older adults now seek professionals who help them nurture productive, rewarding lives. This trend is reflected in the rising need for careers in such areas as retirement counseling, adult education, family relations, and fitness.

Difference in Age Cohorts

It should be noted that the older adult age range—approximately 60 years to 100 years—represents a large and diverse population that cannot be incorporated into an all-inclusive profile on aging. This age group represents an age range of approximately forty years. If we reflect on the developmental changes that occur in the forty years between adolescence and middle age, we see the strong distinction among the characteristics of each developmental stage. The forty-year span from ages 60 to 100 is no less diverse than it is from ages 14 to 54. Nevertheless, a general public that prefers to label all as "senior citizens" in a collective identity disregards this diversity. The 66-year-old and the 86-year-old are both older adults, but they differ greatly in their physical, emotional, mental, and psychological frameworks. One important distinction is that they do not share the same history. It has been said that one's characteristics and attitudes are largely attributable to the social mores and historical events of the era in which one lived. For instance, the 86-year-old who has lived through the Great

Depression will have a different frame of reference, and thus different values, than the 66-year-old who did not experience it. Similarly, the cohort of baby boomers who have lived through such events as political assassinations, wars, and space exploration, will have a different view about themselves and their worlds at age 75 than the 75-year-old adults of today. There is no question that the historical period in which one has lived exerts profound influence on how one looks at one's prospects for aging.

Therefore, the gerontologist must understand that individual needs or behaviors can never be classified by age group. What concerns elders in the year 2010 will not inevitably concern elders in the year 2030. Each older adult is a unique composite of individual, cultural, and cohort influences. In light of this, it is imperative that gerontologists remain current with local, national, and international gerontological practices. This can be accomplished in many ways including interaction with clients and colleagues, research, and affiliation with professional organizations.

Confronting Ageism

Ageism is a prejudicial attitude toward the aged and the aging process. It is reflected in critical views of older adults' behavior, underestimation of their abilities, and ignorance of their needs and desires. It is imperative that future gerontologists examine whether their attitudes and behaviors reflect and perpetuate ageism. Often ageism is so societally inbred that it is difficult to identify and eradicate it. However, a self-evaluation process is essential if the gerontologist is to be effective in her or his work with older adults.

For example, a prevailing ageist attitude is that older adults regress into a second childhood, incapable of adult reasoning and requiring pointed directions on any activity. This is reflected in the patronizing, "sing-songy" quality of some gerontologists' speech to older adults. The clients see through this, are alienated by it, and are inclined to nonparticipation.

Another form of ageism is the misguided belief that frailty and dependency accompany aging, disregarding the fact that the vast majority of older adults are healthy home owners. This ageist view results in funding being targeted to institutional care rather than programs designed to help seniors maintain independent living within their own homes.

Some outdated career guidance textbooks also foster ageism by forewarning future gerontologists that they can expect to have to fight personal depression in their work, as they will be interacting with older people who are in various stages of deterioration! This negative advice is more likely to deter than attract new professionals to the field.

How Do I View My Own Aging?

A basic part of examining prevailing attitudes toward aging is a self-assessment of one's own attitudes toward aging. How one feels about the prospects of one's own aging and the image of what those later years will be like have a direct correlation to the type of attitude one will project to older adults. If one has a basic uneasiness or disdain about the prospects of aging, these attitudes will be projected in one's interaction and work with older clients. Older adults will, in turn, pick up on this negativity and be disinclined to participate. If, on the other hand, one anticipates the later years as a positive time, a more positive rapport with older clients is established. The effectiveness of the working relationship will be directly affected by whether the gerontologist has a positive or negative view of her or his own aging. To better examine how one perceives older adults, the future gerontologist is advised to complete this self-inventory:

1. How do I envision my life at age 60, 70, 80, 90? How do I see myself physically? Emotionally? Socially? Mentally? Economically? What is my living environment?

2. What services do I think I will need? Meals on Wheels? Financial counseling? Employment counseling? Transportation?

3. Do I have any role models of aging? (Describe them.) Why are they role models? How have they influenced me?

4. What are the connotations of the descriptive words I use in referring to older adults (aged, elder, retiree, frail, senior citizen, elderly, mature adult)? Have I seen or heard any other terms that have influenced my perceptions of older adults?

5. What images of aging have I seen in the print and electronic media? Have they influenced my perceptions of older adults? If so, how?

6. What can I learn from older adults? What can I offer to them?

Responses to this inventory reveal the views that the gerontologist will bring into his or her gerontology practice. For instance, if the individual anticipates a later life marked by ill health, it is likely he or she will envision a gerontology career serving the frail elderly.

Preparation to Be a Gerontologist

Motivation to enter the gerontology field often comes from an individual's positive experiences with one or more older adults in her or his life. For instance, having had an inspirational relationship with a grandparent often leads one to seek employment associated with people of that age. Having developed such an enriching relationship, the future gerontologist anticipates a career of working with older adults to be characterized by these same rewarding qualities.

For youth to develop interest in gerontology careers, it is imperative that they have more interactions with older adults through their homes, schools, and communities. Future gerontologists come from those who have grown to admire their elders. This cannot occur as long as the only image that youth have of older adults is through ageist TV commercial portrayals. Through intergenerational programs such as mixed-age choruses or senior tutoring programs, youth receive a more realistic view of older people and eliminate the fears that formerly inhibited social contact. As a result, students are then not averse to considering gerontology or geriatrics as career choices. Students are encouraged to do as much volunteer work as possible, preferably in a variety of settings serving both frail and well elderly, to get a broad overview of career options in gerontology and geriatrics.

The skills necessary for working with older adults will vary depending on the nature of the career. The skills needed for an architect of senior housing are very different from those required of a social worker counseling abused elderly clients. The required technical and interpersonal skills vary considerably. Since the gerontology field is multidisciplinary, it is not possible to outline in this book all of the skills necessary for each gerontology career. Contact should be made with the professional organization in one's field—for example, the National Association of Social Workers—to determine the job-specific competencies, educational background, and work experience required. The appendixes at the end of this book contain listings of professional organizations available to help the future gerontologist in his or her job preparation and search.

Although the skills necessary for each profession are dependent on the nature of that particular work, some universal skills exist by the very fact that each profession shares the commonality of serving older adults. These interpersonal skills and attitudes are essential whether one is driving the senior escort van or administering a nursing home. Since gerontology is essentially a profession involving considerable social contact, the gerontologist should possess strong communication skills. The gerontologist should reflect empathy with and caring for each individual. Patience and flexibility should guide her or his interactions with older adults. Public speaking, computer, and grants-writing skills are valuable assets. The ability to work cooperatively with other colleagues is also essential. More and more, gerontologists are working in multidisciplinary teams in order to maximize the benefits of their service delivery. Therefore, the individual must be receptive to input from others representing a variety of professional disciplines. The most important attribute for any gerontologist is respect for the unique life experience of each older adult; this should be the guiding principle motivating any gerontology career.

Older Adults in the Gerontology Field

Earlier references on career opportunities in gerontology often consciously or unconsciously perpetuated the ageist attitude of "doing for" the older adult rather than "doing with." The idea of hiring older adults themselves to serve their peers was given token attention, if any attention at all. Advice on employment in gerontology careers was directed exclusively to the new college graduate or "second career" middle adult with little regard for the accumulated life experiences of the older adult. It is unacceptable that qualified older adults seeking to fill these positions are turned down due to ageist hiring practices.

There has been concern expressed by many members of the senior community that they are not adequately represented in the labor force hired to serve them. They are not saying that their age entitles them to specialized treatment, merely fair and equal consideration. There are sixteen million Americans age 55 and over who are either working or seeking work. More than a million workers between the ages of 70 and 74 are employed. In 2000 about 12 percent of older Americans were working or actively seeking employment. Approximately 21 percent of older adults reported earnings as the major source of their income; 90 percent indicated Social Security, 62 percent reported income from assets, and 44 percent stated public and private pensions.

There is a widespread perception that gerontology careers are for young and middle adults who wish to "care for" the old. This view establishes a prevailing dependency model that is counterproductive and patronizing. Gerontology careers should be seen as being open to people of any age who wish to contribute their skills toward the improvement of some aspect of the quality of life of older adults. In actuality, older adults themselves are ideally suited for gerontology careers because they can empathize with their clients.

2

CAREERS IN GERONTOLOGY

THE OLDER ADULT population is characterized by great heterogeneity. Older adults live many different lifestyles in many different settings; thus a broad range of gerontology personnel are needed to provide the diverse services older adults require. The central aim of this chapter is to acquaint the reader with these varied occupations and occupational settings within the gerontology field.

Occupational Choices

The following list is representative of existing gerontology careers. The occupations have been listed under general career areas for clarity of reference; however, since most of these occupations would be appropriate to more than one career area, the listings should be viewed in that context. For example, the nursing home ombudsman can be considered a career in advocacy as well as health care.

It should be noted that each of these job titles represents a profession permitting great flexibility and growth. Each of these workers could apply her or his particular training (for example, law, counseling, or medicine) to teaching, research, direct service, administration, private practice, or consultant work. A nurse, for instance, could serve as consultant to an architect who is designing barrier-free condominiums, teach home-care training courses for caregivers of Alzheimer's patients, or administer a visiting nurses program. There are many ways in which any given gerontology profession can serve older adults; it would be well for the gerontologist to remain open to the many contexts in which her or his expertise can be applied.

Advocacy

Adult protective services representative
Community organizer
Consumer advocate
Geriatric consultant
Legislative advocate
Legislative assistant
Lobbyist
Ombudsman
Patient advocate
Social activist
Tenant advocate

Business Administration/Technology

Administrator for state agency on aging
Administrator of a gerontological foundation
Advertiser/marketer of products to older adults
Architect
Consultant on consumer needs of older adults
Director of employment agency for older adults
Editor of a senior publication

Eldercare manager
Engineer
Environmental designer
Grants writer
Industrial gerontologist
Industrial recreation
director
Investment counselor
Life care community
administrator
Manager of senior
housing
Pension advisor

Pre-retirement program
coordinator
Product designer
Program manager of assisted
living facility
Retiree relations administrator
Retirement counselor
Second-career counselor
Senior citizens center director
Senior employment counselor
Senior housing project
manager
Volunteer coordinator

Communications

Advertisement executive
Documentary film maker
Graphic artist
Host of radio or TV
program on senior issues
Magazine writer

Market research analyst
Media watch organizer
Newspaper reporter
Public relations officer
Researcher
Scriptwriter

Criminal Justice/Law

Conservatorship/guardian-
ship program director
Crime prevention program
officer for older adult
unit
Elder abuse investigator
Law enforcement officer
Lawyer

Legal counselor of the elderly
Ombudsman
Paralegal
Program coordinator
Safety lock program
coordinator
Victim/witness assistance
program director

Education

Adult education teacher
Arts outreach coordinator
Caregiver support group coordinator
College/university gerontology professor
Cooperative extension instructor
Computer technology consultant
Continuing education coordinator
Elderhostel coordinator
Geriatric education center director
Gerontology in-service staff training teacher
Gerontology program coordinator
Health educator
Historian
Intergenerational program director
Librarian in older adult services
Literacy program coordinator
Organizer of workshops/ seminars for older adults
Political scientist
Pre-retirement/retirement workshop leader
Researcher
Scientist
Sociologist
Teacher at a senior citizens center or senior residence

Health Services

AIDS educator
Audiologist
Biomedical researcher
Chiropractor
Community health planner
Dental assistant
Dentist
Dietitian
Emergency medical technician
Fire and paramedical staff
Geriatric aide
Geriatric nurse
Geriatric nurse practitioner
Geriatric physician
Health services manager

Health/wellness educator
Home health aide
Home health care provider
Hospice provider
Licensed practical nurse
Long-term care provider
Medical laboratory worker
Medical record technician
Medical social worker
Medical technologist
Nurse's aide
Nursing home administrator/
  ombudsman
Nutritionist
Ophthalmologist
Optometrist
Osteopath
Personal care attendant

Pharmacist
Pharmacy assistant
Physician
Physician assistant
Podiatrist
Public health administrator
Radiation therapy
  technologist
Radiographer
Registered nurse
Residential care/assisted
  living administrator
Respite care program
  administrator
Senior companion
Visiting nurse
X-ray technician

Ministry

Chaplain to nursing home
Director of volunteers
Homebound outreach
  coordinator

Pastoral counselor
Senior services program
  coordinator

Recreation

Fitness instructor
Leisure counselor
Recreation director
  (e.g., retirement communities, senior citizen centers)

Senior travel agent
Wellness center coordinator

Rehabilitation

Activity professional

Arts therapist (art, dance, drama, music, poetry)

Exercise physiologist

Horticulture therapist

Massage therapist

Occupational therapist

Physical therapist

Recreation therapist

Rehabilitation counselor

Respiratory therapist

Speech therapist

Social Services

Addictions specialist

Adult day care center provider

AIDS service worker

Area Agency on Aging administrator

Bereavement counselor

Caregiver support group leader

Case manager

Case worker in adult protective services

Chore services worker

Clinical psychologist

Crisis intervention specialist

Demographer

Director of social services

Economist

Family therapist

Foster grandparent coordinator

Friendly visitors program coordinator

Geriatric consultant

Home attendant

Homebound shoppers program director

Housing counselor

Human services worker

Information and referral specialist

Kinship/foster care/grandparenting support worker

Life skills counselor

Marriage and family counselor

Meals on Wheels coordinator

Mental health counselor

Nutrition site director

Office on aging outreach worker

Outreach coordinator
Policy planner
Private geriatric case
    manager
Psychiatric social worker
Psychiatrist
Psychologist
Rural services provider

Senior citizens center staff
Social worker
Substance abuse counselor
Support group counselor
Telephone reassurance
    outreach worker
Transportation coordinator
Urban and regional planner

Environments in Which Gerontologists Work

Just as there are all levels and types of gerontology careers, so too are there varied settings in which these vocational services are extended. Because the older adult population is composed of both well, active individuals and frail, "at risk" individuals, the environments listed here reflect that contrast.

Community Programs

Academic and other educational and research settings
Advocacy organizations
Businesses and industries
Civic and fraternal organizations
Clubs and social groups
Commercial and private agencies
Community services
County extension offices
Family service organizations

Government agencies (federal, state, county); including the aging network (system of service delivery to older persons established by a federal law, the Older Americans Act)
Human services
Legal services
Media organizations
Municipal recreation agencies

Nonprofit organizations
Professional organizations
Religious organizations
Senior citizens centers

Social service agencies
Transportation
Voluntary organizations

Health Services

Adult day care programs
Ambulatory clinics
Community-based health
  care programs
Health maintenance
  organizations
Home health services
Hospices

Hospitals
Long-term health care
  facilities
Medical clinics
Mental health clinics
Nursing homes/subacute care
Public health programs
Respite programs

Housing

Assisted living facilities
Board and care homes
Congregate housing
Continuing care retirement
  communities

Housing projects
Life care communities
Retirement communities
Shared housing

Gerontology Career Areas

Following is a discussion of some of the primary gerontology career areas in the previous career listings.

Recreation/Leisure Services

In light of the fact that older adults have more discretionary income and leisure time than ever before, there is greater need for recreation directors to assist them in achieving qualitative leisure pursuits.

Research has substantiated that the mental and physical health of elders is enhanced by their participation in social and physical activities. Recreational activities strengthen the elder's ability to maintain independence and prevent illness. The 2002–2003 *Occupational Outlook Handbook* indicates a rising demand for recreation workers in senior citizen centers, retirement communities, and wellness/eldercare programs.

A prominent form of recreation service to older adults is the provision of leisure counseling to pre-retirees and retirees, a service enabling them to determine their leisure values and interests. Corporations or social service agencies may employ these counselors or they may be entrepreneurs with their own private practice.

Another popular recreation career option is commercial recreation, which involves the administration and leadership of profit-making agencies requiring expenditure on the part of the patrons, such as cabana clubs or travel agencies. Travel agents can choose to make older adults their primary clientele, thus creating gerontology careers in tourism.

Other leisure services professionals are trained to work as recreation therapists for older adults with special needs, such as nursing home residents, adult day care clients, elderly inmates, and physically disabled World War II veterans. Recreation therapists provide a diagnostic form of recreation leadership in that they prescribe and evaluate the influence of a particular recreational activity on the physical, emotional, or intellectual health of the older adult. The 2000–2001 *Occupational Outlook Handbook* points to the increasing employment opportunities in recreation therapy in geriatric settings.

Communications

Those in the communications field promote products and services to older consumers. Since the older adult population has become such a large consumer market, vendors more and more are seeking ways to attract them as customers. Those interested in a career in communications should be soundly trained in the realities—not the myths—of aging. Individuals having no knowledge of older adults create far too many insulting media images of old age. This is alarming and destructive, for every time the TV viewer sees an older woman peevishly squeezing toilet tissue rolls for softness, it is not only the product that is being marketed, but more basically, an insulting view of aging that is being perpetuated. This should especially concern parents and educators, since their efforts to foster positive intergenerational perspectives among their children may be seriously impeded by the daily media messages their children receive.

It is encouraging to observe the growing application of media resources to gerontological services. Many communications professionals have chosen to make the elderly the sole focus of their programs. Cable television networks are also making their resources available as a means of community education on aging, showcasing of older adults' talents, and televised study programs particularly welcome to the homebound elderly. Interactive television enables the elder viewer to become an active participant in media events. The gerontology field welcomes such communications personnel as marketing directors, writers, and artists, who are sensitized to ways of improving images of and services to the elderly.

Education

Teachers of gerontology will bring their expertise to a wide variety of professional settings, including research institutes, community or health organizations, adult education programs, industry, colleges and universities, conferences, government agencies, speakers' series, travel programs, and professional associations. By introducing theoretical and programmatic information on aging to a professional group, be it doctors or architects, the teacher aims to have the professionals realize how their practice could be better adapted to serving older adults. Educational sessions are also directed to practitioners, for example, social workers or nurses already serving the elderly, to provide them with resource information that will assist them in their service.

Although the thrust of gerontology educational efforts has been to train gerontologists to fill the many gaps in services, teachers are also needed to introduce gerontology to elementary and secondary school programs. Due to lack of information and a glut of media stereotypical images, children have grown up with a fear of their own aging and a negative view of older adults. This cycle, a damaging one to both the individual and society, can be broken only through gerontology education introduced throughout the public school system. Education on aging can be integrated into any subject area (for example, writing oral histories in English, cross-cultural aging study in world history, media images of aging in art, and study of grandparenting in family studies). Educators can design curriculum materials that correct ageist stereotypes and present factual, candid gerontology information. Intergenerational programs, whereby young people associate with elders in mutual projects, is the ideal way for youth to have their misconceptions corrected.

The educational level of the older population is rising. Between 1970 and 2000, the percentage of those who had completed high school increased from 28 percent to 70 percent. Interest in educational programs for elders increases with each new cohort of older adults as they are exposed to expanded educational opportunities. Learning is now appreciated as a lifelong process, not merely restricted to a person's early years. Gerontologists play an important role in these educational programs as administrators, grants writers, educators, and program evaluators.

Some elders choose to attend college or Lifelong Learning classes on an audit or credit basis for the purpose of career advancement and/or personal enrichment. Institutions of higher education have developed institutes specifically targeted to older adults. These programs offer college-level courses on a noncredit seminar basis. These institutions have included the Institute for Retired Professionals, the Lifelong Learning Institute, and an international term, the Third Age University. Usually older adults design the content of the curriculum and often teach the courses.

The popularity of the Elderhostel movement reflects the widespread interest in education among older adults. Elderhostel offers programs in more than eighteen hundred colleges and universities, museums, conference centers, state and national parks, and environmental centers; more than forty foreign countries host Elderhostel programs. Elderhostelers attend one week of educational programming consisting of three noncredit courses, usually centered on a theme, and enjoy a variety of cultural and social activities. Some Elderhostel weeks are intergenerational, permitting the Elderhosteler to invite a grandchild or young friend. The term "Elderhostel" originated from the concept that participants would live in hostel-like environments, moving on from one educational experience to another, in the tradition of hostelers and life sojourners.

Technological advances have enabled older adults to access educational programs directly into their homes. The television will continue to emerge as an educational medium through expanded cable television and instructional television. Older adults are becoming increasingly computer literate and so are able to utilize distance education formats such as electronic instruction and telecommunication. Distance education is particularly attractive to those who are physically distant from an educational center, as well as those not interested in attending a structured class in a group setting. Gerontologists familiar with the design of distance education are in strong demand.

Illiteracy

Illiteracy is a major problem worldwide and exists among the older adults of this country. One reason why many older adults do not avail themselves of community educational programs is because of poor literacy skills. In America, although at least one-third of those classified as functionally illiterate are older adults, less than 10 percent receive literacy programs.

This low percentage is due to a number of factors. For one, many literacy coordinators focus their efforts on literacy for youth, falsely assuming that elders will not have as much of a need to read as will youth preparing for the workforce. This ageism neglects the fact that many older adults do need to read for all aspects of daily survival (such as reading job applications, street signs, medication bottles, financial statements). Many older adults are exploited because of their inability to read and compute contracts, and many become seriously ill or die due to the fact that they can't read their prescriptions. Reading is not only a vital life skill, it is also a valuable source of satisfaction as an individual leisure pursuit. Reading bridges the generations as grandparents and adopt-a-grandparents read stories to youth.

When literacy programs are targeted to older consumers, they are often not successful. Due to poor or nonexistent reading skills, the elder may not be able to understand any written materials advertising literacy programs. Further, even if the individual is informed of these programs, the feelings of depression, anxiety, and/or shame often accompanying illiteracy can be obstacles to any program attendance.

Gerontologists coordinating and teaching literacy programs for older adults need to be more creative in their outreach efforts and teaching approaches. To increase accessibility, programs should be promoted through the networks common to older adults, such as religious organizations and senior citizens centers. Since many elders are loath to acknowledge their illiteracy publicly, educational programs need to be adapted to the individual, focusing primarily on one-on-one tutoring, often in the home. Reading skills should be applied to life skills such as Bible reading and understanding of Medicare bills. Educators cannot teach reading and mathematics to adults the same way they would to children; their approach and content need to reflect respect for the older learner's life experience. Educational materials need to contain content relevant to the interests of older adults. Gerontologists are needed to create "user friendly" material appropriate for older adults.

Business/Industry

In the year 2005, today's baby boomers will comprise 21 percent of the American workforce, outnumbering younger workers. The fact that the majority of the labor force will be older adults will create a dynamic that industrial gerontologists need to plan for. The growing aging workforce, particularly among women, will necessitate a series of services to be provided by industrial gerontologists. These services include, among others: older worker recruitment and training, retraining in new technological skills involving expanded computer use, retirement preparation, employee benefits, labor policy making, design and marketing of products for older consumers, health promotion, and elder care. Industrial gerontologists are needed in such areas as employment counseling, product development, marketing, retirement counseling, and elder care services.

Companies have increasingly come to recognize the skills of their retirees and are "unretiring" them to return as part-time workers or consultants. There will need to be alternate career path options so that these individuals can make maximum use of their skills in their later years. Variable work patterns will be expanded, including flextime, job sharing, and phased retirement. "Flextime" refers to permitting flexibility in work scheduling; for instance, in one week the worker may work six five-hour days and the next week three ten-hour days. "Job sharing" describes a work situation in which one job is divided between two or more people. In "phased retirement," the individual gradually reduces work time, thus "phasing into" retirement.

Gerontologists in business are increasingly needed as human resources or employee assistance personnel (EAPs). EAPs are committed to keeping their employees well and satisfied and thus more productive. They offer services such as child care and counseling to help relieve the stress in their employees' lives. Because many employees are experiencing physical and mental burnout due to the stress of caring for an elderly relative, their employers are recognizing the need to provide elder care. However, elder care exists in only a small percentage of agencies as of yet; employers have been relatively slow in realizing that the employees' need for elder care is equal to, if not greater than, the need for child care.

Although the care of elderly relatives is shared by family members, most is done by working women, many of whom are also caring for children. The stress of caregiving may result in illness, depression, absenteeism, and either loss of job or change from full- to part-time status. In order to secure their own labor force, employers need to address these problems and the resultant lowered productivity associated with caregiving. Elder care services that they can provide to their caregiving employees include family leave pay, flextime, vouchers for respite/day care and home care, stress management seminars, caregiver support groups, educational seminars, information and referral, counseling, and a comprehensive directory of community resources.

As the number of consumers over sixty years of age continues to grow, the more business vendors will seek out gerontologists to tailor their service delivery to older adults' needs. Gerontologists will be hired as marketing specialists by banks, corporations, insurance companies, condominiums, travel agencies, hotels, retailers, securities dealers, and social service agencies. The 2000–2001 *Occupational Outlook Handbook* projects a 15 percent increase in marketing and sales positions, or 2.3 million jobs; positions in gerontology will be a large portion of these jobs. These gerontologists will be expected to assess the needs of the contracting agency's older clientele and make recommendations regarding the advertising and sale of their products and services to older adults. There are growing opportunities for the employment of gerontologists in the private commercial sector due largely to the fact that older adults are now in a position to selectively purchase services to meet their needs, such as housing and health care. Improved economic and educational resources permit many older adults now to comparatively select from a competitive market of commercial service agencies rather than be restricted to governmentally subsidized social services. Private and commercial health care businesses are proliferating in a service field once restricted to publicly funded programs. For instance, a retirement planning company is usually comprised of financial planners, health care professionals, lawyers, counselors, architects, and administrators who advise elderly clients on such matters as health, housing, financial planning, interpersonal relationships, and leisure and work options.

More and more, financial counselors are being hired to relate exclusively to the older adult's unique needs such as social security, pension rights, annuities, mutual funds, health and long-term care insurance, home equity conversion, and income maintenance

Grants Writing

Foundations, as grant-giving bodies, provide employment opportunities in gerontology. Those foundations with aging as a major focus of their grant giving employ trained gerontologists to review applications. To determine which grants will best meet the needs of older adults, it is essential that gerontologists with knowledge of these needs be responsible for the decision-making process. In addition to the position of a foundation's administrator, there are also many other gerontology career opportunities in the grant field. For instance, agencies often employ grants writers trained in gerontology to write grants that will, in some way, improve the quality of life of older adults. The grants writer can be contracted per project or hired permanently by an agency interested in aging. Some agencies require that their staff members be skilled in grants writing and do not contract or hire a grants writer specifically. Therefore, it is incumbent upon the future gerontologist to develop grants-writing skills.

For each grant application approved, additional gerontology positions are created because staff are needed to implement the grant project. For instance, a grant to initiate a home-delivered Meals on Wheels program would require gerontologists from such fields as nutrition, social work, public administration, and transportation. It should also be noted that grants writing is helpful to entrepreneurial gerontologists interested in initiating or expanding a gerontology careers venture.

There are a significant number of foundations whose major funding interest is the welfare of older adults. To obtain information regarding these grants, individuals should contact The Foundation Center, 79 Fifth Avenue, New York, NY 10003. The following publications are available for purchase from The Foundation Center: *The Foundation Directory*; *Grantsmakers in Aging*; *Grants for Aging*; *Aging—The Burden Study on Foundation Grantmaking Trends*; *The National Guide to Funding in Aging*. Such references are helpful to the grants writer in that they categorize foundations according to those that accept individual or agency grants and those that are restricted to specific geographical areas.

Technology

Technology's impact on society has been dramatic and, as such, has had far-reaching effects on the lives of older adults. The future promises extensive opportunities to employ technology in meeting the needs of older adults. Therefore, gerontology careers incorporating knowledge of technology will be numerous and diverse. Examples of this technology include computers, life-extending medical equipment, and adapted environmental designs, all of which enable older adults to maintain their independence and access vital services.

According to the 2000–2001 *Occupational Outlook Handbook*, employment in computer and data processing will be the fastest growing industry, increasing 117 percent from 1998 to 2008. Computer technicians in gerontology and geriatrics are expected to harness this information technology to provide a quality delivery system that is cost-effective and accessible. There are a variety of positions available in computer systems: computer systems analysts, engineers, scientists, computer support specialists, database administrators, computer programmers, technical consultants, and others. The job horizon is broad for website designers in the gerontology field. Agencies, educational programs, and entrepreneurs realize that the public increasingly seeks its information from the Internet. People with computer skills are needed to bring this gerontology information to the consumer.

The computer is assisting social services staffs in providing decentralized, coordinated care management. Through interactive computing, these staffs are able to engage elder clients in dialogue regarding their conditions. Two-way interactive video enables remote rural health centers and home-care sites to communicate with a central information site such as an urban hospital, thus improving the quality of health care assessment, service delivery, and monitoring. Technology also is expanding opportunities for staff communication and in-service training in such forms as teleconferencing and electronic mail.

Increasingly, older adults are learning how to utilize home computers for educational and recreational use. In 2001, Internet access was present in 3.9 million (17.7 percent) of elderly households, which is 42.6 percent of the general population. About 9.3 million (28.4 percent) older people had computer access. The computer is a significant means of communication between older adults as exemplified by such services as SeniorNet and Senior

Online. Also, the computer provides much information through community bulletin boards, international and national news, consumer markets, and investment information. For those who are homebound or institutionalized, the computer is particularly vital as a link to the community; for instance, significant intergenerational relationships have been established through computer linkups between schools and elders' homes.

Technology has also produced a variety of assistive devices to help maximize the functional capacity of elders experiencing physical or sensory impairment and cognitive or behavioral problems. Robotics allows for daily human functions to be assisted through automation. Assistive self-help devices include corrective lenses, hearing aids, pacemakers, and prosthetic devices. For the hearing impaired, amplification devices can be attached to telephones and telecaption adapters to televisions. Numerous devices are available for those with memory loss, including alarms to signal key locations, appointments, and medication schedules. Due to adaptation of the environment and installation of self-help devices, elders are able to remain in their homes and avoid institutionalization. These aids include, for example, adapted kitchens, lowered lighting fixtures, and specially equipped vehicles such as lift-equipped vans. Medic Alert systems or PERS (personal emergency response systems) are electronic devices that enable an isolated, homebound elder to alert caregivers, police and fire departments, hospitals, and social service agencies in the event of an emergency. The passage of the American Disabilities Act mandates that government-sponsored programs be accessible to individuals with any disability; therefore, gerontologists will need to be familiar with the use of technology in creating physically accessible facilities.

Criminal Justice/Law

The victimization of older adults occurs in many forms and necessitates the response of trained personnel in gerontology careers within the criminal justice professions. Also, elders need assistance with a variety of legal matters, such as the establishment of wills and estates. Elder law, the practice of law with older adult clientele, is increasing as a career choice of lawyers.

Elder Abuse

Statistics show that elder abuse affects approximately two million American elders, but in reality the numbers are even larger; it is estimated that only one in six elder abuse cases is actually reported to the police. Society has largely overlooked domestic violence against the elderly, instead focusing primarily on child abuse.

Elder abuse consists of any of the following:

- physical abuse—use of physical force causing bodily harm (e.g., unreasonable confinement, physical restraint)
- sexual abuse—nonconsensual sexual contact (e.g., sexual molestation or assault)
- psychological/emotional abuse—infliction of anguish, pain, or distress through verbal or nonverbal acts (e.g., insults, threats, intimidation, isolation)
- neglect—refusal or failure to care for elder (e.g., isolation or withholding of companionship, medicine, food, or opportunities for exercise)
- abandonment—desertion of an elderly person (e.g., leaving elder at a hospital)

- financial or material exploitation—illegal or improper use of an elder's funds, property, or assets (e.g., forgery, theft, cashing elder's checks without authorization)
- self-neglect—behavior of an elder that threatens his or her own health or safety (e.g., neglecting medication, ignoring physical hygiene, starvation)

There are three categories of elder abuse:

1. Domestic elder abuse is abuse by someone who has a special relationship with the elder and that occurs in the elder's home or in a caregiver's home.
2. Institutional abuse occurs in a residential facility by someone who has an obligation to care for the elder, such as a caregiver or nursing home staff member.
3. Self-neglect or self-abuse is when the elder refuses to care for himself/herself.

Most reported elder abuse victims are frail, white, middle-class widows over seventy-five years of age. Approximately 84 percent of the abusers are relatives, and 75 percent of the victims live with the abusers. About 30 percent of the abusers are adult children; 15 percent are spouses. Many abusers are financially dependent on the elders whom they abuse.

The abuse springs from many possible causes in the abuser: substance abuse, sexual dysfunction, unemployment, mental illness, extremely low self-esteem, or marital conflict. Often the abuse results from accumulation of caregiver stress, or it is an acting out of some long-standing resentment toward the elder, such as for earlier abuse by the elder. Frequently, elder abuse is an outgrowth of a cycle of abuse in the family; many abusers have been abused themselves in their youth or adulthood and, therefore, view their abusive behavior as normal.

Most often the victims do not report the abuse to the police. This is due to a number of reasons: physical limitations, isolation from the community, internalized shame, fear of abandonment, and dread of reprisal from the abuser in the form of escalated violence, neglect, or institutionalization. In large part, the victims find it difficult to accept that people whom they trusted are actually harming them; others who do face the reality may not report the crime because they still have an emotional attachment to the abusers and do not want to see them subjected to prosecution.

In most states, Adult Protective Services (APS), typically located within the human service agency, is the principal agency responsible for elder abuse investigations; of all of the adult abuse investigations (eighteen years and up) 70 percent of the caseload involves elder abuse.

In addition to APS, there are other settings in which gerontologists can work to eliminate elder abuse. These include: state units on aging; law enforcement (police, district attorney, court system, the sheriff's department); medical examiner/coroner's office, hospitals and medical clinics; state long-term-care ombudsmen's office; public health agency; area agency on aging; mental health agency; facility licensing/certification agency; agencies providing information and referral; and hot lines (e.g., long-distance caregivers can call a nationwide toll-free Eldercare Locator number, 800-677-1116, to locate services for the elders in their care).

The tragedy of elder abuse points to the growing need for trained gerontology personnel in many fields. Social services staffs are needed to work with families to prevent the development of elder abuse. If the signs of potential elder abuse are there, professional intervention is required to prevent the abuse. For instance, an unemployed, addicted son living with his elderly mother has the potential to abuse her by stealing her Social Security checks for drugs and beating her when he is in a drug stupor. Social service workers can also offer caregiver support groups and counseling to minimize the possibility of caregivers letting the pressures of their daily roles escalate to violence toward the elders they are supposed to be protecting. In the event of danger and abuse, adult protective services staff may need to be brought in. Housing workers must develop "safe homes" for abused elders; these sanctuaries have been created for battered women and children, but few are provided for elder victims. Law enforcement personnel will be called to respond to the abuse of elders. Educators will be expected to train the general community to identify and report the existence of elder abuse in their communities.

Legal Matters

Lawyers are involved in elder abuse cases and in other legal matters affecting older adults. A growing number of attorneys identify themselves as elder-law attorneys because they address solely the needs of elder clients. Their legal cases include: age discrimination in employment; consumer fraud; tenancy problems; finances related to Social Security, Medicaid, Medicare, Supplementary Security Income, unemployment insurance, disability insurance, estate planning, and pensions; nursing home or home-care violations; spousal impoverishment; bioethical disputes; protective services; living wills; and guardianship and conservatorship cases. ("Guardianship" refers to the designation of a guardian in the event that the elder is declared legally incompetent to manage personal affairs. "Conservatorship" involves the appointment of a conservator to assist a legally competent elder with business decisions.) County and local bar associations provide a number of services to older adults including: legal rights and benefits handbooks, community education on legal issues, advocacy and legislative training for community groups, and pro bono legal representation.

Lawyers, as well as correctional officers and social workers, are recognizing that they need gerontological background to work with older adults convicted of offenses. The crimes committed by older adults range from shoplifting to homicide. Incarcerated elders consist of three groups of people: those who have been imprisoned for the first time after the age of sixty, those who have been in and out of the prison system throughout their lives, and those who have aged in prison with sentences of ten or more years. Research and understanding of the unique needs of incarcerated elders is sadly lacking. Researchers, policy makers, and direct service personnel need to be acquainted with the physical, psychological, emotional, and social aspects of aging so as to appropriately respond to older inmates.

As an alternative to the legal process, mediation programs are being established as a means of resolving disputes. A mediator is trained by a lawyer to serve as a neutral third party to facilitate communication between disputants. Through mediation, the disputants arrive at a negotiated agreement, thus avoiding court costs and legal entanglements. Mediation is particularly relevant to the legal concerns of older adults, for it is used in disputes involving such subjects as nursing homes and home care, age discrimination, estate planning, guardianship and conservatorship, pensions, family disputes, landlord/tenant conflicts, and consumer complaints.

Mediation projects occur in such settings as housing complexes, senior citizens centers, dispute resolution centers, legal services, attorney generals' offices, and offices of long-term-care ombudsmen. Referrals come from many sources including courts, churches, social service agencies, and offices of therapists and attorneys. Mediator training is open to any staff or volunteer, but older counselors are strongly encouraged to become mediators on issues relating to their peers. The disputants are more likely to be receptive to a mediator who is their peer; in turn, the older mediator is likely to relate to the issues raised by the disputants. Through the Older Americans Act, Area Agencies on Aging were funded to provide legal assistance for financially needy elderly. Due to the availability of mediation centers that are able to address lesser complaints and offenses, the Area Agencies on Aging have been able to reserve these funds to help elders pay court costs for serious legal cases.

Police departments have recognized the need to provide targeted services to older adults and to train their personnel in gerontology. Police crime-prevention units can provide community education to older adult groups on such topics as elder abuse and home safety. Older adults are particularly susceptible to fraudulent schemes; for instance, the FBI indicates that older adults are the largest group targeted by nearly one hundred illegal telemarketing operations. There have been many examples nationwide of elders being tricked out of money for phony repair or investment deals. They are also victims of predatory lending practices. Criminals take advantage of the trusting and/or vulnerable qualities of their elder victims. Law enforcement officials are putting increased emphasis on arresting the predators as well as educating senior citizens to the potential for this victimization.

Police understanding of such conditions as Alzheimer's disease is essential. It has been found that the cause of much elder spouse abuse is due to the violent behavior of some Alzheimer's patients. These patients, disoriented and aggressive, do not recall inflicting harm on their spouses. The spouse caring for the Alzheimer's patient can also become violent as caregiving stresses mount. Police have also responded to the problem of wandering Alzheimer's patients by establishing a detection system whereby they can identify and return the patients to their homes.

Police departments have crime-prevention units, some with a specific office for senior services. The work of crime-prevention units includes such activities as escort services, installation of safety devices, and the establishment of block crime watches. There is growing recognition that crimes can best be prevented or their effects minimized if police work in multidisciplinary teams with other professionals. These crisis intervention teams involve medical personnel, adult protective services staff, the office on aging employees, prosecutors, and police, all of whom apply the unique skills of their individual professions toward the common goal of protecting the security of older adults.

Victim assistance programs are operated out of most prosecutors' offices in order to provide supportive services to victims, such as counseling, transportation to court, and relocation. Coordinators trained in gerontology are best equipped to relate to elder victims; in fact, elders who are former victims are strongly encouraged to become peer counselors. Victim assistance programs should be in a location accessible to older adults, such as a commonly frequented senior citizens center or religious institution.

Research reveals that there is actually less physical victimization of older adults than other age groups. However, this is no comfort; any level of crime is unacceptable. The feelings of lone-liness and vulnerability that can accompany the aging process become especially acute when one views her or his environment to be life threatening. This fear of crime produces a chain of responses that seriously reduces the older adult's quality of life. As a form of protection, the individual often literally lives in dread behind locked doors. Not benefiting from social interaction, the individual frequently suffers depression. In being isolated from the community, he or she is shut off from needed social services. Thus, the individual literally becomes one of the homebound, not because of a physical handicap or lack of transportation, but because the fear of crime has immobilized her or him emotionally.

Health Services

Health care must be viewed as a continuum involving health main-tenance, disease prevention, medical treatment, and aftercare. Unfortunately, the term "health care" has connoted hospitaliza-tion for a physical illness; instead, it should be viewed as a wide range of services addressing both mental and physical health needs. There are many geriatric professions along this continuum. The health careers listed earlier in this chapter reveal a broad range of positions from paraprofessional jobs (home health aide) to jobs requiring advanced degrees (biomedical researcher). According to the 2000–2001 *Occupational Outlook Handbook*, health services is among the largest and fastest growing service industries; by 2008 there are expected to be 2.8 million jobs in the health services field. The strongest areas of employment are managed care, health maintenance organizations (HMOs), home health care, residential care, offices, and clinics. Other positions are in hospitals, nursing homes, government agencies, social service agencies, and medical labs. These positions will include both the administrative aspects of health care, such as finance, as well as the clinical sphere encompassing such areas as nursing and counseling.

There has been a growth in careers related to maintaining and ensuring the health and wellness of older adults. This growing emphasis on health education is reflected in the improved health of each succeeding cohort of elders. For instance, the decline of heart disease, the former number one killer of older adults, can be partially attributed to the public's greater attention to proper nutrition, exercise, and medical care. Health/wellness services are provided by a variety of gerontologists including nutritionists, fitness instructors, and arts therapists working in a diversity of settings such as community centers, health spas, and industrial recreation programs. People are increasingly subscribing to the practice of holistic health care, realizing that the integration of positive mental attitude, healthy diet, and sufficient exercise prevents the occurrence of later physical problems. There is also increasing interest in alternative and complementary therapies, resulting in new gerontology employment opportunities. Also, as health information continues to flood the media, gerontologists are hired to help elder consumers access the information relevant to their individual needs. As seniors live longer and also become more educated, they are demanding more information and services related to healthy lifestyle choices, disease prevention, and treatment options.

In the gerontology field, there is a great need for workers to help older adults manage their expenditures on health care and navigate the health insurance maze. In 1999 older Americans spent 11 percent of their total expenditures on health (insurance, drugs, medical services, and medical supplies). Since nearly one-third of older

Americans, or eleven million, lack any form of drug coverage, gerontologists are needed to provide financial advisement. Gerontologists will be particularly helpful in assisting elders with Medicare and Medicaid paperwork. Medicare provides insurance coverage to those over sixty-five; for those income eligible, Medicaid covers some level of supplemental health coverage for 5.9 million beneficiaries, including prescription drug coverage, nursing home care, and more. As baby boomers age, the subject of age-based entitlements will be questioned; due to their large numbers, older adults may only receive benefits based on financial need, not age.

All gerontology professionals should be well acquainted with the physical losses that can accompany aging so that they are able to distinguish psychological and emotional problems from physically induced ones. For example, hearing loss or blurred vision may result in feelings of withdrawal or defensiveness. A hearing aid or glasses may thus eliminate the psychological distress.

A person's physical health has a direct impact on his or her mental and emotional stability. Poor nutrition, for instance, can lead to disorientation and lethargy, which can be incorrectly interpreted as mental illness. Nutritional deficiencies can be prevented through a number of interventions including nutrition counseling, transportation to congregate meals and supermarkets, correction of denture problems, elimination of substance abuse, financial aid, assistance with mobility within the home, and creation of a social environment more conducive to meal enjoyment. Nutritionists can advise clients on the prevention and treatment of common ailments such as diabetes or heart disease. Dietitians provide meals tailored to the medical needs of each individual. Nutrition screening is now recognized as essential for disease prevention, resiliency in recovery from illness, and the eradication of malnutrition.

The importance of a healthy lifestyle to prevention of illness is illustrated in the following cycle: osteoporosis, the lessening of bone mass, can be offset through lifelong nutrition, exercise, and possible medication. Osteoporosis is a leading cause of hip fractures that, by the year 2030, are expected to cause long-term disability in four hundred thousand people. The hip fracture may lead to poor mobility and possible entry to a nursing home. The physical disability can lead to depression, thus creating mental health problems that in turn can exacerbate physical illness. The cycle could have been prevented had attention to wellness been part of the lifestyle.

The National Safety Council reports that each year about twenty-six thousand people over sixty-five die from accidental injuries, and at least eight hundred thousand others sustain injuries resulting in short- or long-term disability. Attention to physical and mental conditioning helps in the prevention of such accidents. One-third of nursing home admissions is caused by mobility problems that might have been averted through health and wellness efforts throughout the life span. Gerontologists address this need by working as designers of home safety products and home safety auditors.

Falls are the most common injury to the elderly. Hearing and visual impairments, poor physical conditioning, depression, osteoporosis, drugs, and alcohol usually cause them. Among elders aged sixty-five to seventy-four, motor vehicle accidents are the most common forms of accidental death due to diminished coordination and slower reaction time. If the older adult adopts a lifestyle that develops greater stamina and physical coordination, the individual is less likely to be vulnerable to falls and car accidents.

The leading cause of death among persons sixty-five or older was heart disease, cancer, stroke, chronic obstructive pulmonary diseases, pneumonia, influenza, and diabetes. Sex and race distinguish varying mortality rates. In 1997, among elders, diabetes was the third leading cause of death among American Indian and Alaska Native men and women, fourth among older Hispanic men and women, and sixth among older white men and women and older Asian and Pacific Islander men.

There is a shortage of geriatricians to meet the needs of the elderly population worldwide. There are less than 25 percent of the number of geriatricians we need in America; by the year 2030 we will need thirty-six thousand geriatricians. Geriatricians will be expected to assume more responsibility for community education on health issues and aging. For instance, the Omnibus Reconciliation Act of 1990 (OBRA) created the first legislative mandate that pharmacists provide counseling to clients. Also, the demand is great for researchers to develop cures of conditions commonly occurring in old age (for example, heart disease, cancer, stroke, and Alzheimer's disease). Geriatric-assessment training needs to be a part of all medical training. Since emergency rooms have become the sole source of medical care for many elderly poor, ER staff training is particularly critical. Staff in Veterans Administration hospitals also will require more geriatric education.

Nurses, R.N.s and L.P.N.s, will be in strong demand in geriatric work. R.N.s assess residents' needs, develop treatment plans, and serve as administrators and supervisors. L.P.N.s are employed to provide bedside care, administer medications, supervise nursing assistants, and attend to a variety of personal and health care needs of the client. Nursing aides, also known as nursing assistants, geriatric aides, or hospital attendants, are supervised by medical staff and assist in a variety of personal and health care activities such as eating, walking, or blood pressure readings.

All health care professions will flourish in this geriatric boon. Physical therapists assist those recovering from injury or illness to achieve physical stability. Occupational therapists are employed to assist clients in carrying out activities of daily living such as dressing or feeding. Speech therapists help the older client with speech and hearing challenges associated with aging and/or illness. Due to the prevalence of respiratory ailments among the elderly (pneumonia, chronic bronchitis, emphysema, and heart disease), respiratory therapists will be in demand. Dietitians provide nutritional counseling and prepare meals appropriate for each client's dietary and health needs. Medical directors are needed to ensure the efficacy of medical services. The list of job opportunities in geriatric health care is an extensive one and includes, for example, ophthalmic technicians, pharmacists, dental lab technicians, radiologic technologists, opticians, clinical lab workers, surgical technologists, emergency medical technicians, cardiology technologists, medical record technicians, and biological and medical scientists. Within each career area, there are also opportunities for people to be employed as assistants, for example, pharmacy assistants and physical therapy assistants.

Regarding mental health services, older adults have been seriously shortchanged in that only a small number of those needing mental health treatment receive it. Depression, the most common form of mental illness in the elderly, is not receiving adequate treatment. Some depression is situational (related to widowhood or retirement, for example); other symptoms reflect an intense, long-term condition defined as clinical depression. Gerontologists working as policy makers, administrators, and counselors need to eliminate the serious gaps in mental health services for the elderly. They must stop viewing old age as a debilitating period that naturally brings on depression; depression is not a corollary to aging, but rather a mental illness that can and should be treated by mental health professionals.

The Demand for Gerontologists

The over-eighty population will continue to be the fastest growing group of elders. Since these individuals are living longer, usually with some chronic illness, there will be increased demand for gerontologists in the health services. A large proportion of the elderly have one or more chronic health problems, including diabetes, heart disease, hypertension, arthritis, osteoporosis, incontinence, oral/dental problems, nutritional deficiencies, and visual and hearing impairments. Few report that these conditions inhibit major activity. However, as people live longer, their chronic conditions can become more severe, resulting in increased demands on the health care system to provide long-term care. Current projections are that there will be eleven million dependent older persons by 2040.

Long-Term Care

"Long-term care" is defined as a continuum of care that includes a range of health and residential services. Long-term care includes subacute, rehabilitative, medical, skilled nursing, and supportive social services for people who have functional limitations or chronic health conditions and are in need of ongoing health care or assistance with normal activities of daily living. Long-term care includes nursing homes and a variety of other settings such as respite care and adult day care. Long-term care administration is a $50 to $100 billion industry, second only to hospitals.

In managed care, there has been a shift from fee for service (FFS) systems to managed care networks—Health Maintenance Organizations (HMOs) and Provider Organizations (PPOs). This shift has been driven by the demand for cost control and more provider choice to ensure quality care. Today more than sixty million Americans are enrolled in some type of HMO. By 2005, 30 percent of Medicare recipients are expected to be enrolled in managed care. To help seniors navigate this bureaucratic maze, there is a need for gerontologists in a number of roles including managed care caseworkers, data entry personnel, and policy analysts.

Nursing homes are intended for those who require twenty-four-hour medical supervision. At the present time, there are 16,400 Medicare/Medicaid certified nursing homes and 1,000+ private facilities. Medicare long-term-care services are covered by Part A, "Skilled Nursing Facility" (SNF) services associated with postoperative or posthospitalization including rehabilitation therapies. Medicaid "Nursing Facility" (NF) services are provided to state residents who meet Medicaid eligibility requirements. About 1.56 million older adults or 4.5 percent of seniors over 65 live in nursing homes; 1.1 percent of those are age 65 to 74, 4.7 percent are 75 to 84, and 18.2 percent are 85 or older.

This rise in institutionalization is due to a number of factors: (1) inadequate funding of home-care alternatives, (2) rise in population with chronic illness, (3) increase in number of individuals living alone (particularly women) with no family to assist with basic needs, (4) early discharge from hospitals precluding time necessary for seeking alternatives to a nursing home, and (5) longer life span of single women requiring expanded services. The majority of nursing home residents have some form of mental disorder, but little care is provided within the nursing home. The average pro-

file of a nursing home resident is an eighty-four-year-old white widow, with only a 50 percent likelihood of having any living (and visiting) friends or relatives, an average of four diseases, and a national average stay of thirty months. Nursing homes are convalescent health centers. Although many patients do remain permanently in their nursing homes, a number may also return to the community after recuperating from a physical or mental problem.

Contrary to public perception, the nursing home is not solely an age-segregated environment for older adults. Nursing homes treat individuals of all ages through their subacute-care units. These special care units are designated for patients with a specific need for treatment (for example, AIDS, Alzheimer's disease, head trauma, dialysis, Huntington's disease, ventilator care, and children's disability). Nursing homes, now often called care centers or convalescent centers to better represent their diversity of services, may have one or more subacute-care units. Subacute-care units provide such services as intravenous therapy, cardiac rehabilitation, wound management, chemotherapy, general nursing, and pulmonary care. Subacute care is a thriving development in the post-acute-care industry. Since Medicare's Prospective Payment Systems (PPS) pay hospitals only a fixed amount for a specific illness, post acute care in the hospital has been discouraged. Therefore, there has been a push to discharge patients to subacute care, which costs 20 to 60 percent less than hospital care. Health care analysts indicate that 10 to 20 percent of those currently being treated in hospitals could be transferred to subacute care. It is estimated that subacute care has the potential to be a five to twenty billion dollar market for nursing homes. Nursing home staff will require training in how to relate to the needs of these diverse populations in their facilities. Not only will understanding of the various illnesses be required, but also a willingness to explore types of intergenerational programming.

Today there are approximately thirty thousand licensed nursing home administrators. Over half of nursing facilities are part of a chain of facilities owned or leased by a multifacility organization. The average cost of nursing home care per year is $40,000. Medicaid patients are subsidized for nursing home care; since many Medicare patients cannot afford nursing home costs, many actually eliminate their assets or "spend down" to reach Medicaid eligibility. Medicaid pays for nearly 40 percent of nursing home care and 16 percent of home and community-based care. Medicare reimburses 9 percent of nursing home costs for stays up to one hundred days and 54 percent of home care. Nearly one-fifth of home care is paid for out of pocket. The limited allocation of home health care funds in favor of institutional funds actually fosters unnecessary nursing home placement. An alarming commentary on this situation is that 40 percent of those in nursing homes needn't have been placed there if there had been sufficient funding for home health care alternatives and if they had been appropriately diagnosed and treated by a trained geriatrician. The statistic is frequently noted that only 5 percent of older Americans are in nursing homes at any one time. Although this statistic would appear encouraging due to the fact that the majority can then be said to be active in the community, the figure cannot really be viewed as positive because as indicated above, 40 percent of that total need not be there if there were home-care alternatives.

Among older adults, home-based health care is preferred over institutionalization in a nursing home; it is understandable that they would prefer to remain in their own surroundings. As a result, there has been a demand for home health care workers and home-care workers. It is important to note the distinction between home health care and home care as these terms have incorrectly been used interchangeably. Certified Home Health Care Aides (CHHAs) assist clients with activities of daily living (ADLs) such as bathing, dressing, and toileting, and medical procedures such as tube feeding and lesion irrigation. These aides usually provide such care under the direction of a nurse, although certain medical procedures may have to be administered solely by a nurse. Most home health aides are employed by home health agencies, visiting nurses associations, social service agencies, residential care facilities, nursing facilities, hospitals, public health agencies, and community volunteer agencies. CHHAs will be the fastest growing occupational group among health providers. Rehabilitation and chronic care needs will be met at home due to a number of factors: the client's preference for the home environment, the availability of technology allowing home care, and the financial pressure to release patients from hospitals and nursing homes. Home-care attendants or aides, also referred to as homemakers, are not qualified to provide health services; rather, they assist clients with instrumental activities of daily living (IADLs) such as housecleaning, laundry, shopping, meal service, and paperwork assistance. In short, home health care aides do not do housework and home-care attendants do not do medical procedures.

The personal care aide (PCA), however, is an individual whose level of care is between that of the home health care aide and the home-care aide. PCAs provide ADL assistance (toileting, bathing) and IADL assistance (laundry, shopping) but not health care (medication, blood pressure). In addition to CHHAs, PCAs, and home-care aides, a number of other gerontology careers comprise this community-based, noninstitutional care network; they may include, among others, telephone reassurance workers, chore service staff, friendly visitors, and providers of home energy and home weatherization funding.

Other gerontologists provide supportive environments that permit the care recipient to receive therapeutic stimulation and the caregiver to receive a break from care. One such environment is adult day care, a day program providing health, social, and related supportive services to frail older adults while the caregivers work. There are two types of adult day care. An adult day health center (ADHC) serves those who require more medical intervention. ADHCs are usually conducted in nursing homes or hospitals. The social day care center, on the other hand, is for higher functioning elders than those who would attend an ADHC; its focus is on socialization, and it is normally conducted in senior citizens centers, social service agencies, and religious organizations. Some adult day care programs are designed to serve one primary clientele, such as Alzheimer's patients.

A variety of housing options also enable the individual needing some personal care to remain in the community rather than enter an institution. Today there are about 45,000 residential care/assisted living administrators and more than 1,000 continuing care administrators. Over the last fifteen years there has been a steady increase in the number of community based alternatives to nursing homes. There are approximately 40,000 congregate/residential care living facilities, 15,000 family care homes, 5,000 assisted living facilities, and 1,000 life care or continuing care retirement communities.

Board and care homes, also called personal care homes, are managed homes providing ADL assistance. Assisted living facilities (ALFs) are similar to board and care homes but are usually larger and provide more health care. ALFs are in a variety of settings: they may stand alone or they may be part of a life care or continuing care community, nursing home, housing complex, or hospital. Residential health care facilities (RHCFs) are ALFs under the supervision of nurses. Life care communities (LCCs) provide independent, semi-independent, and dependent living environments for residents, thus providing the security of lifetime care. For an initial fee and monthly payments, the resident has the lifetime assurance of services as needed, including home health care, respite care, nursing home care, social services, nutritional counseling, meals, and transportation. The continuing care retirement community (CCRC) differs from the LCC in that it does not require an up-front payment for projected lifelong services, but rather entails payment for services as needed. The costs of CCRCs and LCCs generally restrict their availability to only middle-to-upper-class individuals.

Another environment providing community based care is respite care, which offers care to the care recipient while the caregiver takes a respite, or rest, from caregiving responsibilities. Respite services are similar to those offered in the adult day care programs; the distinction is that the care can extend for overnight, weekend, or longer periods. Unlike the adult day care, which runs on a day-to-day schedule, the respite program is designed to provide extended care. Respite programs are usually operated out of a nursing home or hospital.

Another service within the health care continuum is the hospice, which serves the terminally ill and their loved ones. The purposes of hospice are to assist the individual in dying with dignity and in comfort and also to help families and friends through the caregiving and bereavement process. Pain management is a critically important part of the geriatrician's hospice services. There are more than 2,000 hospice programs in America; most are in independent community programs, with the remainder in hospitals, home health agencies, and nursing homes. A major strength of the hospice movement is the use of the interdisciplinary team to more comprehensively address its clients' needs. The interdisciplinary team incorporates the skills of many gerontologists; it consists, for example, of a social worker, physician, pastoral counselor, bereavement counselor, nurse, physical therapist, occupational therapist, and trained volunteer.

Social Services

Gerontology careers in social services represent many professional areas, as outlined in the earlier list in this chapter. There are a variety of careers including, among others, tenant advocate, information and referral specialist, social worker, counselor, and crisis intervention specialist. Gerontologists in social services work in a variety of settings with individual elders, their families, and with groups of elders. They are involved in direct service, community education, advocacy, teaching, research, and policy development.

Aging brings with it a spectrum of emotional and psychological changes. Depression is common to many in later life. To safeguard the mental health of the elderly, counselors who have been trained in gerontology are needed. In recognition of this need, the American Psychological Association has created a new concentration entitled clinical geropsychology. Curriculum content includes the social, psychological, and biological aspects of aging; psychopathology; diagnostic assessment; and intervention and legislative initiatives. Research by the Andrus Gerontology Center reveals that fewer than two hundred doctoral-level and counseling psychologists have older adults as their primary clientele; this reflects a critical shortage as societal projections reveal that there will be a need for five thousand geropsychologists by the year 2020.

Gerontologists in social services work to improve the quality of life of the elderly in many ways. For example, as a result of the 1975 Older Americans Act, every state has a long-term ombudsman program created to investigate and resolve complaints of care in nursing homes, residential health care facilities (RHCFs), adult day health centers, board and care homes, and VA hospitals. Adult protective services staff (APS) serve mentally and physically impaired elders by providing legal, social, and medical services that enable them to remain in the community. Another program to prevent institutionalization is adult foster care, in which vulnerable elders are placed in the care of individual families. Geriatric social workers are increasingly called to address the needs of the mentally challenged and developmentally disabled; as individuals live longer with these conditions, they provide a new challenge to gerontologists. Also, gerontologists must address the needs of elders who are themselves caregivers of mentally challenged, developmentally disabled children. As the sole caregivers of their dependent children, these elders experience great physical and mental stress, including anxiety as to who will care for their children after they die.

Geriatric care managers assist elders and their families access necessary services. After conducting a client needs assessment, the care manager makes necessary referrals to appropriate community resources such as home care, subsidized transportation, and visiting nurses. Private geriatric care managers, often self-employed entrepreneurs, are frequently employed as long-distance caregivers by family members who do not live near their elderly relatives. These family members count on the private geriatric care manager to keep in regular contact with their elders and to relay their observations to them via phone or electronic mail. In addition to private practice, hospitals and health maintenance organizations also employ geriatric case managers.

Gerontologists are also engaged in expanding elders' knowledge of and usage of social services. Insufficient transportation services limit the accessibility to necessary services for older adults. Forty percent of older adults don't drive, and mass transit is often costly, unsafe, and not in close proximity. In their social services positions, gerontologists arrange for rerouting and assistive devices in mass transit, subsidized fares, and the scheduling of community vans to transport older adults to appointments and community events.

Social services for older adults are often provided in settings that are nonthreatening and psychologically accessible to them. This is done in the understanding that elders are more likely to avail themselves of counseling in a familiar social atmosphere than in a separate clinic. It is for this reason that the senior citizens center is often a focal point for the delivery of social services.

The senior citizens center, an example of a community program, is a multipurpose center providing a variety of services, including counseling, health services, recreation and education programs, employment assistance, financial counseling, information and referral, nutrition programs, social action, tenant advocacy, transportation services, consumer education, volunteer opportunities, and legal aid. The participants of senior citizens centers acknowledge them as essential to mental, emotional, and physical health. Many senior citizens centers also use their resources to reach out to the homebound elderly. Homebound services extended from the center include delivery of Meals on Wheels, telephone reassurance programs, friendly visiting companion programs, transportation/escort services, counseling, chore assistance by a homemaker, basic nursing assistance by a home health aide, recreation counseling, physical therapy, and home repair. Homebound adults receive similar services from hospitals, business firms, public health departments, professional associations, church groups, service clubs, and county offices on aging.

Recognizing that not all older adults are physically able or psychologically willing to visit social service offices, mobile outreach teams consisting of health and social service staffs bring the needed services to elders right in their homes and immediate neighborhoods. Gerontologists also train peer counselors, recognizing that older adults are in a unique position to assist each other through such commonly shared experiences as widowhood, grandparenting, and job seeking. Peer counselors can be trained to be I&R (information and referral) specialists to provide clients with contacts and resources appropriate to their needs and requests.

In their capacities as social workers, case managers, counselors, and other gerontology workers, gerontologists also train the community to assist in identifying the social service needs of older adults. The term "gatekeeper" has been used to describe those community representatives who are often the only point of contact with isolated elders. These gatekeepers, which include mail carriers, utility workers, house managers, meal deliverers, police, and firefighters, are increasingly being trained by gerontologists in methods of assessing and responding to the needs of vulnerable elders. For instance, a meter reader may observe the accumulation of unread newspapers and empty liquor bottles in an elder's home; if appropriately trained, he or she will know to make a report on this observation to the county office on aging.

Within social services, gerontologists also work as economists and social scientists. Social action and political involvement are major aspects of many older adults' lives. This is reflected in the fact that the largest voting block in this country is represented by those between the ages of fifty-five and sixty-four. Groups like the Gray Panthers fight against such problems as age discrimination, health care costs, defense spending, and pollution. Older adults should have a higher representation among legislative bodies.

The 2000–2001 *Occupational Outlook Handbook* states that geriatric social work will continue to be the highest area of employment for social workers. They are employed in a variety of settings, including rehabilitation centers, nursing homes, substance abuse treatment programs, adult day care centers, residential facilities, hospices and clinics, among others. Businesses also recognize the importance of gerontologists in ensuring quality service to their senior customers; social workers are employed in such sites as banks, investment firms, corporate eldercare firms, unions, and public guardian services. The social worker has many options for employment in gerontology and geriatrics.

Housing

There are many positions for gerontologists in the housing field including housing managers, policy analysts, architects, financial counselors, and retirement counselors. These positions can occur in private industry, nonprofit organizations, or on an individual consultant basis. Architecture is a high growth gerontology profession as demand continues for community based alternatives to hospitals and nursing homes. Accompanying the rise in these units will be growth in employment of housing property managers and food service managers. Gerontologists trained in business are needed to acquaint elderly home owners with such options as home equity conversion, chore assistance, home repair, energy assistance, and weatherization. Social service coordinators in senior housing units are needed to assist residents in obtaining needed services.

In America, a little more than one-half of older adults live in nine states (California, Florida, New York, Texas, Pennsylvania, Ohio, Illinois, Michigan, and New Jersey). The diversity of older adults' living environments reflects the diversity of the older adult population itself. There are many factors considered in the choice of housing, including proximity to family and friends, nature of health, geographical limitations, local resources, economics, and weather. Two-thirds of people over seventy-five own their own homes and wish to remain doing so. Most are women who live in metropolitan areas and are less likely to change residence than other age groups. The Department of Housing and Urban Development reports that 1.5 million people live in housing that exceeds their income level, is substandard, and fails to accommodate their physical capabilities or assistance levels.

Most older adults want to remain in their homes as they age, a lifestyle defined as "aging in place." However, 90 percent of older adults live in single family homes that do not meet their physical needs. Among elders, six out of ten falls in the home are the result of hazards and obstructions. About 1.14 million elders have heart and mobility problems, and as such, are in need of architectural modifications to their homes. These modifications include, for example, ramps, widened hallways, grab bars, and handrails. The addition of such assistive devices, coupled with overall improvements in long-term health, has resulted in increasing numbers of elders able to maintain independent living.

Even with home modifications, some older adults require more supportive services and need alternate housing options. These include, for example, retirement communities, congregate housing, shared housing, accessory apartments, and senior housing complexes.

A retirement community is a large, age-segregated, residential development offering such support services as recreation, transportation, maintenance, and security. Retirement communities provide no health care services and are geared for the active, well elderly.

"Congregate housing" (congregate care facilities or CCFs) is defined as a group residence of self-contained apartments providing supportive services, such as housekeeping, meals, transportation, and recreation. "Shared housing," sometimes intergenerational, describes a living environment in which two or more unrelated people share common areas of a home. Shared housing consists of three types: a home sponsored by an organization such as a county office on aging or religious group, the rental or purchase of a home by two or more individuals, or a home owner's rental of his or her own home to a tenant who may provide chores in exchange for housing.

An "accessory apartment" is a private living unit attached to a home. An older home owner may rent the accessory unit in order to have additional income and/or caregiver assistance; also, a family may design the accessory unit for an elderly relative who wishes to be nearby but still maintain independence. Elder cottage housing opportunities (ECHO), or "granny flats," have the same characteristics as accessory units, with the exception that they are not attached to the private home but are removable units placed on the property of the home owner.

Some housing projects are designated as subsidized housing for older adults and provide meals and transportation to residents. Other housing projects become naturally occurring retirement communities (NORCs) because the residents "age in place" in the complex and become the predominant age group. Housing managers of these NORCs have recognized the need for social service assistance to these elder residents and have sought out gerontologists to work as social workers, case managers, and I&R specialists. The American Association of Homes for the Aging (AAHA) offers a national certification program for retirement housing professionals. Core courses include Administering the Retirement Housing Community, Management and the Aging Resident, and Managing the Financial and Physical Environment.

Homelessness is a condition increasingly affecting older adults. Over 25 percent of the homeless in America are over the age of sixty. Because pensions and Social Security cannot keep up with inflation and rent costs, many find it impossible to pay for the rent and upkeep of living quarters. Due to these factors, as well as the lack of federally funded housing or transitional shelters, many older adults become homeless. Physical disability and substance abuse exacerbate the vulnerability of the elderly homeless.

A large number of the homeless are mental patients released from institutions. The decision to deinstitutionalize these individuals is praiseworthy, acknowledging that an institution is not the best place for rehabilitation and healthy living. However, homelessness has occurred due to the fact that few alternate community mental health care programs were initiated to serve those reentering the community. As a result, many of the homeless are disoriented individuals unable to cope with basic daily life decisions. Since many of the elderly homeless have spent most of their lifetimes in institutions, their unsupervised discharge into the community is particularly traumatizing. Gerontologists can work for housing reform through such positions as social policy and legislative analysts, media journalists, and advocates.

Ministry

Those employed within religious organizations will be expected to enhance their service delivery to older adults. People training for the ministry will have to learn about the needs of older adults and develop congregational responses to those needs. Ministry to older adults includes, among other aspects, outreach to homebound elderly and services to nursing home residents and hospitalized elders. Religious organizations also provide older adults with various opportunities for creative and spiritual growth, such as educational and recreational programs and volunteer opportunities.

Since aging services are strengthened by interagency cooperation, it is important that religious organizations link with other community agencies in the provision of services. For many older adults, the church or temple is their primary source of information, more so than the local media or senior service agencies. Clergy have significant influence on their congregations; if they announce a community program for seniors, there is a strong likelihood that the elders in the congregation will attend. In addition to expanding social services to older adults, religious leaders also assume a significant role on ethics teams, which assess the ethics and morality of various health care decisions impacting on elderly patients.

Advocacy

Gerontologists as policy makers in social services are those who help conceptualize the visions that will be implemented through specific programs and services. Policy makers are concerned with all aspects of the quality of life of older adults. Therefore, they will work to effect progressive policies in every field including, for example, health care, housing, and labor. These gerontologists may be employed by governmental, commercial, private, or nonprofit agencies.

Policy makers are in a critical position to correct inequities within the older adult population. For instance, policy makers need to establish policies that will reduce economic imbalances. In 2000 about 3.4 million older persons lived below the poverty level; the national poverty rate for the elderly was 10.2 percent. Another 2.2 million older adults, or 6.7 percent, were classified as "near-poor," meaning at incomes less than 25 percent above the poverty line. Poverty continues to impact primarily on older women, minorities, the nonmarried, rural elderly, and those over eighty-five. Of those over eighty-five, 23 percent are near-poor. Among nonmarried seniors, 25 percent are near-poor. About 35 percent of women who never married are near-poor.

The economic security of older adults could be improved through such policy measures as long-term care insurance, pension portability, and financial assistance to caregivers and parenting grandparents. Reduction of prescription costs is another aim of the advocate, for seniors pay for the highest priced medications. The prices paid by seniors have risen faster than the rate of inflation. Were it not for Social Security, 39 percent more older people would be in poverty, with 49 percent of those being over age eighty-five. Policy makers are expected to advocate for seniors in reference to such issues as Medicare, Medicaid, Social Security, Older Americans Act, Adult Protective Services, and the Americans with Disabilities Act. These gerontologists recognize that policies must be developed with an appreciation of global aging and the needs of minority elders. Policy makers work in conjunction with legislative bodies to ensure the enforcement of their policies. They work with administrators and direct service staff to see that these policies are implemented through programs and services. They are increasingly being asked to examine whether funding should be granted according to age-based or needs-based guidelines. It should be noted that the age at which one is termed an "older adult" is variable and is determined by various program policies (for example, age sixty-five for Medicare eligibility and age fifty-five for Elderhostel eligibility). Consequently, there is considerable latitude in determining what age constitutes the entry to older adulthood and later life.

A major source of policy recommendations has been the White House Conference on Aging (WHCOA) in 1961, 1971, and 1981. At these conferences, older adult consumers and gerontologists developed policies that formed the agenda for services over each ensuing decade. The White House Conference on Aging for 1995 focused on the following policy recommendations:

1. to increase public awareness of the interdependence of generations and the essential contributions of older individuals to society for the well-being of all generations,
2. to identify the problems facing older individuals and the commonalities of the problems with problems of younger generations,

3. to examine the well-being of older individuals including the impact the wellness of older adults has on our aging society,

4. to develop such specific and comprehensive recommendations for executive and legislative action as may be appropriate for maintaining and improving the well-being of the aging,

5. to develop recommendations for the coordination of federal policy with state and local needs and the implementation of such recommendations, and

6. to review the status and multigenerational value of recommendations adopted at previous WHCOAs.

The Government's Aging-Services Network

The aging-services network is composed of federal, state, and local agencies that are prime providers of services to older adults. These agencies are major sources of employment for gerontologists. Jobs in the government's aging-services network involve many types of skills including advocacy, research, negotiation, public relations, community organization, personnel management, health care, public health administration, program development and evaluation, needs assessment, data collection, and social service planning.

The government agency most prominently involved in provision of services to older adults is the Administration on Aging (AOA) under the Department of Health and Human Services (HHS). It serves many functions in its pivotal coordinating position, including research, advocacy, direct service, policy development and monitoring, program planning, training of gerontology faculty and practitioners, and curricula development.

AOA was established in 1965 as the federal agency responsible for implementing and overseeing services mandated in the ten original rights of the Older Americans Act. These rights include:

1. adequate income
2. best possible physical and mental health
3. suitable housing
4. full restorative services
5. employment without age discrimination
6. retirement with health, honor, and dignity
7. participation in civic, cultural, and recreational activities
8. community service
9. immediate benefit from research
10. freedom and independence

Structurally the AOA is currently composed of approximately 57 State and Territorial Units on Aging (SUAs), more than 225 Native American organizations, more than 27,000 local providers, and 655 Area Agencies on Aging (AAAs). Each AAA is a public or private agency designated by the state to carry out the AOA's policies on a local level. Since each AAA is involved with older adults on a decentralized, community based level, it is in an ideal position to assess the needs of the area's older adults. These needs are documented in an annual area plan, which is forwarded to the SUA. From the requests submitted by the AAAs, the SUA determines the amount and type of funding needed in the state and makes that request to the AOA.

SUAs and AAAs have their own national associations. The National Association of State Units on Aging (NASUA) includes all state units on aging that disseminate training and program models. The National Association of Area Agencies on Aging (N4A) is composed of AAAs, advisory council members, service provider agencies, and private sector representation. It provides technical and administrative assistance to AAAs in response to federal legislation and regulations.

Because it relies heavily on learning the unique needs of each AAA's older population, the AOA safeguards that funding will go to sources of real human need. Since AOA's mandate is to service those elderly with the greatest economic or social need and strongest likelihood of institutionalization or public dependency, the input from the local communities through the AAAs is essential to determine priority service needs. Following is an outline of the services provided to older adults through the AOA network.*

Services to facilitate access
transportation
outreach
information and referral
client assessment and case management

Services provided in the community
congregate meals
multipurpose senior centers
casework, counseling, emergency services
legal assistance and financial counseling

---

*National Association of State Units on Aging. *An Orientation to the Older Americans Act.* Revised edition. Edited by Susan Coombs Ficke. Washington, D.C.: (July 1985), p. 62.

adult day care, protective services, health screening
housing, residential repair and renovation
physical fitness and recreation
pre-retirement and second-career counseling
employment
crime prevention and victim assistance
volunteer services
health and nutrition education
transportation

Services provided in the home
home health, homemaker, home repairs
home-delivered meals and nutrition education
chore maintenance, visiting, shopping, letter writing,
    escort, and reader services
telephone reassurance
supportive services for families of elderly victims of
    Alzheimer's disease and similar disorders

Services to residents of care-providing families
casework, counseling, placement and relocation assistance
group services, complaint and grievance resolution
visitation, escort services
state long-term care ombudsman program
other community services, as available

AOA also offers service grants to social service agencies and academic institutions in such subject areas as long-term care, elder
abuse prevention, transportation, services to elders with develop-

mental disabilities, mental health, financial counseling, arts therapies leadership, training of practitioners in gerontology, and development of gerontology faculty and curricula. NASUA's National Clearinghouse on State and Local Older Worker Programs provides training and technical assistance to gerontologists managing employment programs for older workers.

3

Challenging the Stereotypes—Challenging the Profession to Respond

Basic to any consideration of employment in gerontology must be a clear, factual understanding of the characteristics of the older population. The misconceptions and myths on aging have kept many people from entering the field. For those who have entered gerontology careers, the quality of their service has often been inadequate and even detrimental because these negative stereotypes have caused them to treat older adults in inappropriate ways. The purpose of this chapter will be to present factual information on aging, which is critical to the effectiveness of any gerontologist.

Senility

Myth: People become senile as they age. Forgetting things means an older adult is getting Alzheimer's disease.

Facts: Senile dementia, the progressive loss of memory and other cognitive functions after the age of sixty-five, affects some but not the majority of the elderly. The tragedy of senile dementia is not fully understood by the public, as evidenced by such facetious, casual comments as, "Old people are depressing; they're senile and always in the past," or "Gramps forgot where he left his keys; Alzheimer's, you bet!"

People of all ages have at some points in their lives temporarily misplaced their keys; it is only when someone is over sixty that this is assumed to be a sign of senile dementia. Society's propensity to label elders as senile or as sufferers of Alzheimer's has become so pervasive that, tragically, many older adults have started to believe the labels, and once they internalize this belief, they begin to fear their own aging. Gerontologists, as teachers and policy makers, must provide the public with sound gerontological information so that the present societal ignorance and resultant damage to older adults is eliminated.

Dementia results from a condition known as organic brain syndrome. This condition—evidenced by such symptoms as disorientation, severe loss of memory, emotional imbalance, and poor reasoning—is identified as either organic brain syndrome (irreversible) or acute brain syndrome (reversible). Chronic brain disorders refer to psychotic disorders that are caused by cerebral arteriosclerosis (insufficient blood to the brain due to hardening of the arteries) or by senile dementia and senile brain disease causing dissolution of the brain cells.

When dementia occurs, it is not restricted to the over-sixty population; presenile dementia is defined as dementia occurring to those under sixty, senile dementia to those over sixty. There are many causes of senile dementia (Parkinson's disease, multi-infarct dementia [MID], Huntington's disease). However, 50 percent of senile dementia is caused by Alzheimer's disease, which currently afflicts four million Americans; by the year 2050 the numbers are expected to rise to a staggering fourteen million. Approximately 10 percent of Americans over sixty have Alzheimer's disease; 40 to 50 percent over eighty-five have the disease. However, the disease has struck people as young as forty. More than 50 percent of nursing home patients are Alzheimer's disease victims. The disease is progressive and degenerative with a duration extending from five to twenty years.

Alzheimer's disease is characterized by memory and intellectual decline, disorientation to time and place, impaired judgment, speech difficulty, personality change (hostility, paranoia), behavior change, and loss of bodily functions. Wandering, sleeplessness, and hallucinations may also occur. The stages of Alzheimer's disease vary with each individual; all of the symptoms outlined above are not present in each patient. Alzheimer's disease destroys crucial parts of the brain. The immune system is attacked and death usually occurs due to a secondary infection such as pneumonia. There is no confirmatory diagnostic test for Alzheimer's disease. To eliminate other possible causes of senile dementia, it is necessary to conduct thorough medical, neurologic, psychiatric, and neuropsychological assessments. It is only through an autopsy that Alzheimer's disease is confirmed; study of the patient's brain cells reveals the presence of abnormal deposits or plaques as well as clumps of nerve fibers. A genetic component has been identified, but currently there is no confirmed cause of Alzheimer's disease and no cure.

Since diagnosis of chronic brain syndrome is so prevalent, it is imperative that comprehensive educational programs on the characteristics of chronic and acute brain syndrome be required of any gerontologist. This involves the mobilization of many fields of gerontology. For instance, educators in college, continuing education, and medical clinics should present the instructional material. Nutritionists should provide information on the role of diet in the prevention and treatment of acute or reversible brain syndrome. Pharmacists can take the same approach on the correct use of medication.

Alzheimer's disease is a debilitating disease devastating to both victims and their families. Research scientists must continue to pursue eradication of chronic brain syndrome and Alzheimer's disease. Institutional and home health care service providers will be in demand. Social workers and counselors will be expected to use their skills in helping Alzheimer's patients cope with the physical and psychological assaults of their progressive deterioration. In addition to providing ongoing counseling in family support groups, social workers will arrange for such services as home-care assistance, respite and day care programs, care sharing among families, and tax deductions for in-home care, all of which are aspects of long-term care planning for this chronic illness.

Educators are needed to acquaint staff and caregivers with the characteristics of Alzheimer's disease, the appropriate methods of response, and how to access community services. For instance, to reduce patient's agitation and confusion, caregivers should reduce stimuli such as verbal directions, diverse colors, and loud sounds. Also, the use of stories, music, images, and objects that trigger reminiscence is encouraged, since long-term memory remains stronger than short-term memory. Architects as consultants and designers create nursing home units appropriate to Alzheimer's patients (for example, color-coded doors and hallways, circular hallways, personalized images on room doors). They also "safety proof" and adapt homes in which Alzheimer's patients live with caregivers.

The Alzheimer's Disease and Related Disorders Association (ADRDA) is an invaluable resource to gerontologists and informal caregivers in its many forms of service including research, advocacy, support groups, training, and educational materials.

Although Alzheimer's disease—a chronic brain syndrome—is irreversible, acute brain syndrome can often be reversed through proper treatment; there are many such reversible conditions. In acute brain syndrome, the psychotic behaviors can be due to any number of treatable causes including thyroid imbalance, dehydration, anemia, lung disease, depression, drug interaction, vitamin deficiency, congestive heart failure, malnutrition, infection and resultant fatigue, strokes, head trauma, substance abuse, and emotional instability due to change or loss.

As many as 50 percent of all older patients may have treatable disorders and can be expected to improve if treated promptly. For instance, it may be only a matter of proper diet to eliminate the incoherent speech misdiagnosed as chronic brain syndrome. All too often a misdiagnosis of chronic brain syndrome leads to an unnecessary treatment that actually creates the chronic brain syndrome that never existed before.

Sexuality

Myth: Older adults are not (or should not be) sexually active.

Facts: Older adults indicate that they place high significance on the role of sexual intimacy in their lives. Many acknowledge that their sexual interest and satisfaction is strong. Older adults have a full appreciation of the many dimensions of love and sexual expression, with intercourse being only one aspect of that fullness; for instance, touching, hugging, and kissing reflect affection and sexual expression as well. In intercourse between older adults, orgasmic pleasure and fulfillment exist. Though the male erection may be slower and ejaculation weaker and the women's vaginal walls thinner and vaginal lubrication less, lovemaking is satisfying and enjoyable.

Older adults' attitudes towards sexuality need to be viewed in the context of their individual lifestyles and societal influences. For instance, if an individual has been sexually active throughout his or her life, it is very likely that the individual will be sexually active in later life; this is an illustration of the continuity theory of aging. A reflection of societal ageism is the belief that attractiveness and sexual potential decline as one ages; in fact, sexuality among older adults is denied, dismissed, frowned upon, and even ridiculed.

Many individuals think that they have to hide their sexual activity from family and friends, fearing their rejection. Some even deny their sexuality and reject relationships due to the intensity of the pressure from family and friends. Some elders have convinced themselves that sex at their age is wrong, having internalized the myth that sex is only for youth and/or for the purpose of procreation.

Some older adults choose to abstain from sex because they feel that some physical condition, such as a vasectomy or hysterectomy, will reduce their sexual desire and ability. A recipient of bypass heart surgery may believe that sexual activity can even be fatal. Informed medical professionals are needed to help allay these fears and concerns.

Gerontologists, through their work in health care, media, education, and counseling, are in a position to provide healthy, accurate information on the beauty and potential of sexuality and aging. Architects of the living environments of older residents can also reverse the trend of designing facilities that prohibit sexual activity between consenting adults.

Sexuality in later life is represented by many different lifestyles: some individuals are in marital relationships, some are in nonmarital but monogamous relationships, some have more than one sexual partner, and some are celibate. Some are homosexual (10 percent of those over sixty) and others are heterosexual. The needs and desires for love, companionship, and intimacy are universal and no less important in later life. Gerontologists need to work out of a philosophy that respects those needs and desires, not thwarts them.

AIDS

Myth: AIDS is a disease that does not impact older adults.

Facts: AIDS is an insidious disease that cuts across all ages; in fact, it has affected the older adult population more than is recognized. More than thirty-three thousand Americans over the age of fifty have AIDS, the terminal stage of HIV infection.

Because society denies the existence of sexuality in older adults, it does not acknowledge that they, in fact, could contract the HIV virus through sexual transmission. The most prominent cause of HIV/AIDS infection among older adults is homosexual activity and bisexual activity; the highest rate of heterosexual transmission of AIDS in America occurs among those over fifty. The second highest cause is exposure to contaminated blood transfusions prior to the mandated blood testing in 1985. Transmission through infected drug needles is the least common cause. Since HIV symptoms can appear as long as ten years after initial infection, older adults can be diagnosed with HIV infection based on sexual activity, IV drug use, or blood transfusions occurring in their pasts.

AIDS education and treatment programs have not been directed to the elderly but have focused primarily on youth. This neglect of elders' needs is due to the false perception that AIDS does not affect the elderly. If older adults continue to be ignored in HIV prevention efforts, they will continue to not take the precautions necessary. Research has shown that, because older adults have not been educated to the fact that they can be infected, they do not use condoms and are less likely than youth to undergo HIV testing.

The lack of HIV testing also is due to the fact that doctors do not prescribe the test for older adults, because they misdiagnose HIV symptoms as Alzheimer's disease. Yet AIDS is clearly distinguished from Alzheimer's disease by its faster progression, greater weight loss, and the absence of aphasia (speech disturbance). Because many doctors mistakenly associate fatigue, disorientation, or illness in elders as "natural outcomes of aging," they do not recognize that these symptoms may be an indication of AIDS.

The AIDS epidemic affects older adults not only as patients but also as caregivers. Many elders are in the tragic position now of caring for children and grandchildren who are HIV infected. With grandchildren orphaned by AIDS, these grandparents assume the parenting role. Sadly, oftentimes the children have inherited the HIV infection from their parents.

Caregiver support group directors, bereavement counselors, and hospice workers assist elders in caring for and grieving for their loved ones who have been afflicted by the HIV virus. Since many nursing homes now designate AIDS units as part of their provision of subacute care, nursing home staffs need to be knowledgeable in the care and treatment of AIDS patients.

Caregiving

Myth: Most families "dump" their physically dependent elderly relatives in nursing homes, with little regard for their welfare.

Facts: On the contrary, research reveals that 80 percent of care is provided by relatives who wish to provide personalized care to their loved ones. Every effort is made to help the care recipient maintain his or her independence at home and avoid institutionalization. When the level of medical care needed cannot be provided at home, the caregiver seeks nursing home options. When care recipients enter nursing homes, it is usually when they have become highly impaired, require twenty-four-hour care, and have multiple problems. In fact, 80 percent have been recently hospitalized and come to the nursing home almost directly from the hospital.

In rank order, wives, husbands, then adult daughters, daughters-in-law, and sons provide most care. About 75 percent of the caregivers are women with an average age of fifty-five to sixty; one-third are over sixty-five. Many of the caregivers who are sons and daughters are also called the "sandwich generation" because they are "sandwiched" between the needs of caring for both children and parents. Full-time working women are four times more likely than men to be the primary caregiver for an elderly relative. Most of the "sandwich generation" is made up of working mothers who, due to caregiving pressures, often cut their work hours from full- to part-time.

The role of older adults as caregivers themselves has not been sufficiently acknowledged in gerontological research. However, it is a fact that it is not uncommon for a 68-year-old woman to be caring for both her 72-year-old spouse and 88-year-old mother. Also, many elders are caring for their ill or disabled children or grandchildren.

Caregiving can incorporate many levels of care (shopping, meal preparation, intravenous therapy, medication monitoring). In most cases, the responsibilities are extensive and time consuming. Three-fourths of caregivers live with their care recipients; 20 percent have provided caregiving for five or more years. Caregiver research has revealed high rates of depression, fatigue, stress, illness, substance abuse, family conflict, and employment complications.

Gerontologists from various professional backgrounds are needed to assist caregivers. For example, nurses, working out of hospitals and clinics or as private consultants, can train caregivers in home health care and personal care. This training can be individualized in the home or conducted in community education programs. Caregivers need information on topics like biopsychosocial aspects of aging, problem solving, anger and stress management, and the utilization of community resources. Mental health counselors can provide individual counseling and support groups to caregivers who are experiencing the stress and emotionalism of caregiving. They can also equip caregivers with valuable resource information such as contacts for day care, respite, and home health care. Respite workers provide a respite from the caregiving and can work within the home or in a health care facility. Eldercare coordinators in the caregivers' work sites can also provide supportive services to their employees.

Suicide

Myth: The age group having the highest rate of suicide is the adolescent population.

Facts: The suicide rate is higher among white males over eighty than in any other group in the nation. Over the past two decades, there has been a tripling in the suicide rate in this age group of males. Of all reported suicides in this country, over 25 percent are committed by older adults.

Suicide among older adults is due primarily to one or more of the following causes: depression, failing health, social isolation, economic problems, substance abuse, and feelings of loss (for example, of independence, roles, loved ones). The American Association of Suicidology indicates that older adults have more completed suicides than younger people do; the ratio of attempts to completed suicides is 4:1 in older adults and 100–200:1 in youth. The association attributes this to the fact that elders use more lethal methods and generally feel a greater motivation to die.

The medical community and allied health professionals have educated the public to warning signs of suicide in youth without also highlighting the staggering level of suicide among the elderly. In addition to expanding their community education efforts, these gerontologists will be expected to increase their crisis intervention teams and mental health outreach efforts to identify elders evidencing potential for suicide.

Productivity

Myth: Older workers are not as effective as younger workers are. In fact, they are a liability.

Facts: Research proves that compared with younger workers older employees are more productive, are absent less frequently, and have fewer accidents on the job. The job skills, motivation, and reliability of older workers are substantiated in investigative studies. By 2005, those fifty-five and older will be nearly 20 percent of the workforce. However, ageism is as prevalent in the workplace as it is everywhere else. Most employers continue to underestimate the potential of the older worker.

Older adults seeking employment encounter obstacles not experienced by other age groups. These obstacles are due to society's ageist view, which serves to block equal access to job opportunities. The abilities of the older adult are questioned; the abilities of youth are glorified. Often older adults will not be trained in the new technology because the employer assumes that they can't learn or keep up. Also, there is the built-in assumption that the older adult should be content to settle into a retirement lifestyle and income, intent to volunteer rather than work for pay. Much of this reasoning is derived from the prevailing attitude of "making way for younger blood" or "giving youth its place in the sun." Further, it is a crude economic fact that some employers want to save money by paying for a fledgling rather than for a lifetime of experience. The elimination of mandatory retirement has not eliminated the very forceful societal undercurrents discouraging employment of people over sixty. Lawyers defending older adults cite violations against the Age Discrimination in Employment Act to be the most pressing legal concern confronting this elder population nationwide. ADEA prohibits age discrimination against people over forty related to hiring, firing, and retirement practices.

Substance Abuse

Myth: Substance abuse is a critical problem among youth, but not among older adults.

Facts: Substance abuse—the intentional or unintentional abuse of drugs and alcohol—is more widespread among the elderly than realized. In some cases, the substance abuse is a conscious choice by the individual; in other cases, it is an "inadvertent addiction," whereby changes in the individual's lifestyle and body metabolism result in a developing dependency.

Inappropriate use of medication among the elderly is common. The average elderly patient is given thirteen varieties of pills a year, most often by specialists who may not know what medication other specialists have dispensed. Without monitoring, a drug interaction is likely to lead to a life-threatening reaction. The number of hospitalizations precipitated by adverse drug reactions is 50 percent higher in elderly patients than it is for those younger than sixty. Another major problem in pharmaceutical service for the elderly is inappropriate dosages. The standard medication dosage is designed for an adult age eighteen to fifty-five with the body metabolism to integrate that dosage. Older adults, on the other hand, have fewer functional units with which to absorb, detoxify, metabolize, and excrete the medication at the same pace. Therefore, the medication has a stronger impact than it should by the very fact that it remains in the bloodstream longer.

Older adults may become addicted to drugs because of the prevalence of polypharmacy (use of multiple drugs). Drug-related problems may account for up to one-third of hospital admissions and one-half of nursing home admissions. Barbiturate overdose is the most common form of suicide.

As with drugs, alcohol metabolizes more slowly in the body as one ages. Therefore, though an individual may have been able to have two to three drinks at a time as a young adult without any adverse reaction, the same two to three drinks taken in later life can cause a physiological and psychological dependency. It is estimated that 10 to 15 percent of older Americans are alcoholics. Two-thirds of these would be described as early onset alcoholics, meaning that they have abused alcohol for most of their lives. One-third would be later-life alcoholics whose destructive drinking is usually a reaction to losses in later life (for example, widowhood or failing health).

Drugs and alcohol can be used as escape from depression; poor mental health often leads to substance abuse. The damage to the body is extensive. Substance abuse also increases the likelihood of falls or vehicular accidents. When drugs and alcohol are mixed, the consequences can be fatal. Creating such a deadly mixture can be an intentional suicide attempt. In other cases, the individual is ignorant of the fact, for instance, that prescription drugs should not be taken with liquor.

Treatment of substance abuse in the elderly is limited partly by the difficulty of detection. Unlike younger addicts, whose substance abuse would evidence itself in poor work performance or a DWI (driving while intoxicated) conviction, the older adult is often retired from work, driving infrequently, and not in social situations where his or her drinking behavior would be noted. For instance, many drink alone, or if they drink socially, it is in the context of a socially accepted happy hour with peers who are also alcohol abusers. Friends and family members often become enablers to the alcoholic's behavior by denying or minimizing it. They do so for a number of reasons. Some have the ageist view that later life is a depressing period, and so their loved ones should be able to escape it through drinking if they so wish. "What other joy does she have?" they might conclude. Others feel shame at their elders' drinking, while others want to deny that their own abusive drinking has strong parallels to that of their elders.

Medical personnel often fail to identify an elder's physical or mental problems as indication of substance abuse, because ageism and insufficient geriatric education often lead them to consider these symptoms merely as inevitable signs of aging. Even if the chemical dependency is identified, treatment responses for elderly substance abusers are lacking. Little priority is given to the rehabilitation of older adults, as society does not give equal value to the lives of the elderly compared to those who are younger. Substance abuse treatment programs do not sufficiently attend to the unique needs of the older substance abuser, such as determining the causes of late onset alcoholism.

There is debate as to whether older substance abusers are best treated in age-segregated programs among their peers; however, there is also concern as to whether their needs are being met in the prevailing models of age-integrated programs. Most abusers do not avail themselves of any treatment program because of physical disability, lack of transportation, avoidance of group situations, denial, and/or shame; the most promising mode of treatment would appear to be through mobile outreach services to their homes.

In the gerontology field, there is a need for educators and health professionals to raise awareness of the severe problem of substance abuse in the elderly. These gerontologists need to develop more comprehensive, successful methods of preventing, identifying, and treating the growing chemical dependency among the elderly.

Retirement

Myth: Retirement triggers physical and mental decline.

Facts: Retirement research reveals that the transition to retirement is usually a smooth, satisfying one, determined in large part by the existence of good health, good finances, and good attitudes toward retirement. There is a trend toward freely chosen earlier retirement accompanied by the retirees' anticipation of a rewarding leisure lifestyle. In those cases, however, where the individuals have chosen early retirement to pursue alternative careers or have been ultimately pressured to retire through employer buyouts, downsizing, and early retirement incentives (ERI), the prospects are less optimistic due to the pervading discriminatory attitude toward employing older adults. It takes longer for an older adult to obtain a job, and at that, it is usually for less money than a younger counterpart would make. In recognition of the job placement difficulties of older adults, gerontologists are administering employment programs targeted specifically to older job seekers. These programs include vocational counseling, training classes (including retraining in technological advancements), and job placement services.

Increasingly, gerontologists are being hired by corporations interested in providing comprehensive pre-retirement programs incorporating economic, legal, and leisure resource guidance for their older workers; financial counselors, lawyers, leisure counselors, and industrial recreation directors are sought by these corporations.

Administrators are attracted by the cost-effectiveness of such programs; profits expand due to the fact that the older workers' productivity increases in direct proportion to the morale boost they experience from the individualized attention these programs provide. If the pre-retirement program educates older workers to the attractive features of retirement, participants are more inclined to elect early retirement, leading the corporation to save on pension costs and lower salaries paid to replacements with less experience.

As older adults' preparation for and interest in retirement has increased, so also has the need for specialized counselors in the various facets of the retirement lifestyle. Second-career counseling and volunteer counseling will continue to assume greater prominence as retirees seek assistance in productive use of their expanded leisure time. These positions can be established under the auspices of corporate personnel departments or as individual consultant businesses. Corporations employ counselors to assist pre-retirees in locating volunteer opportunities, not only because of concern for the welfare of their employees, but also because it is wise public relations. For instance, in providing release time for the pre-retiree to volunteer her or his skills in the local hospital or library, the corporation is enhancing its community relations image.

For some older adults, volunteerism has been a large part of most of their lives; for others, retirement is a period in which to explore a whole new volunteer role. Some, on the other hand, determine that their financial obligations necessitate that they seek jobs instead of volunteer positions. Those who choose to volunteer can do so through government sponsored programs (for example, Foster Grandparent, Retired Senior Volunteer Program), a number of which have income guidelines and offer a low stipend. Many more individuals volunteer in independently initiated or community organized projects. For instance, one may personally choose to do chores for a frail elderly relative. Another may do the same type of homemaker assistance through a placement by a senior volunteer agency. Since volunteerism is a significant part of most older adults' lives, volunteer coordinator positions will continue to exist in many settings (for example, senior citizens centers, county offices on aging, commercial human resources departments). Entrepreneurs conducting retirement planning programs will assist clients in exploring both work and volunteer options.

Counselors are increasingly recognizing that there needs to be a broader view of retirement; the current definition of retirement as a discontinued role in the paid workforce ignores the fact that many women have been full-time unpaid laborers in the home. With domestic responsibilities lessened and children out of the home, these homemakers experience a "retirement transition" just as real as that of the paid employee. In light of such factors, counselors have begun to replace the term "retirement" with such titles as "life transition" or "third age" to acknowledge the diversity of working conditions and lifestyles among older adults.

This portion of the book has provided you with information enabling you to deliver more effective gerontological services. It is an exposure to the field that should encourage you to explore the varied facets of aging through deeper research. The true gerontologist not only possesses the information and skills pertinent to her or his discipline but also has a comprehensive, progressive view of aging that filters through all of her or his work. As a future practitioner, it should be your task through study and critical theory to continue to build that enlightened foundation.

4

TRAINING FOR CAREERS IN GERONTOLOGY

SINCE THE GERONTOLOGY profession incorporates many occupations, as illustrated in Chapter 2, there is no central curriculum appropriate to every gerontology career. Some paraprofessional jobs such as housekeeper/home-care worker or senior transportation driver do not require an academic degree. Other positions such as family therapist or nursing home administrator require at least a bachelor's degree. There are also jobs that require master's or doctoral degrees, such as medical scientist or chairperson of a university gerontology program. There is no standardized license or certification to become a gerontologist. The professional credential is determined by one's career choice. For instance, social workers and nurses have distinct licensing and certification procedures. As is to be expected, the diversity of career opportunities in gerontology is reflected by the diversity of gerontology training requirements.

Educational Programs

Gerontology training can be pursued in noncredit, continuing education programs or in academic programs at the associate's, bachelor's, master's, or doctoral levels. There is no accreditation of academic gerontology programs; however, many subscribe to the standards and guidelines established by the Association for Gerontology in Higher Education (AGHE). AGHE is the only national gerontological organization devoted exclusively to advocacy and information dissemination regarding gerontological education.

AGHE is the most comprehensive, current source of information regarding gerontology training options nationwide. To obtain a list of academic institutions offering programs suitable to one's individual interests, each registrant submits a completed search form to AGHE's computerized National Database on Higher Education. AGHE's *National Directory of Educational Programs in Gerontology and Geriatrics* describes more than one thousand gerontology programs (credit and postdoctoral); more than five hundred of the three thousand institutes of higher education in America offer them. In the directory, these programs are listed by academic level and type of program (major/degree, certificate, or minor/concentration/specialization/emphasis). A job bank listing is also available on the AGHE website.

Gerontology majors, certificates, and minors exist on the associate's, bachelor's, and master's levels. The more advanced the academic level, the greater the emphasis on research, theory, and administration.

In a gerontology major or degree program, the student studies gerontology as the primary academic area. In a certificate program, gerontology is pursued as an adjunct to another field of study, such as business, nursing, or social work. In certificate programs providing academic credit, the certificate is granted following completion of approximately twenty to thirty credits of course work, including the standard requirement of college research papers and exams. The certificate can be pursued in conjunction with another degree or following receipt of a degree. Credit-bearing certificates attract students who wish to focus their studies on issues related to older adults. For instance, a graduate student of architecture may pursue the gerontology certificate because of interest in working in environmental design of life care communities. Similarly, a vocational counselor may obtain a gerontology certificate to be equipped with the knowledge to add retirement counseling, second-career counseling, and eldercare to his or her professional services.

The gerontology minor, also called a concentration, specialization, or emphasis, is a sequence of gerontology courses pursued in conjunction with a complementary academic major such as psychology, social work, or nutrition. For instance, by majoring in music therapy and minoring in gerontology, the student would be well prepared to be a music therapist for an adult day care program or Alzheimer's subacute care unit. The more diversified the training, the more marketable the student will be. For instance, in applying for a position as a senior citizens center director, the individual with a gerontology major and business minor would be a stronger candidate than would be an applicant who has only a business degree. Students may also study gerontology, not as a degree or major, but as a specialization within a traditional discipline or profession (for example, architecture, psychology, medicine, or biology).

Degree programs may be defined as gerontology, aging studies, or human development. The associate degree is offered at a community college and can be applied to a bachelor's degree. The associate degree prepares the individual for entry-level jobs and serves as on-the-job advancement. Generally, the associate's and bachelor's gerontology majors, certificates, and minors lead to entry-level gerontology positions, while master's and doctoral gerontology majors, certificates, and minors lead to management positions as administrators, policy makers, and planners. On the bachelor's level, many colleges and universities offer a degree or certificate in gerontology, or a certificate, minor, or specialization in aging to complement a traditional academic major. Field experience is usually required. The B.A. or M.A. gerontology degree usually has a liberal arts emphasis, while the B.S. or M.S. degree tends to focus on the occupational and/or research applications of gerontology. M.S. degrees that focus on health gerontology, long-term care, nursing home administration, or gerontological nursing may also be designated as M.S. degrees in health services administration, public health, or nursing (for example, training for a geriatric nurse practitioner). Other M.S. degree programs have a specialization or track in long-term care administration, nursing, human services, mental health, research, or gerontological social work. In many master's degree programs, universities offer graduate specializations that permit students to major in another academic or clinical field with a specialization in aging. Nearly one hundred universities offer a master's degree in gerontology. Master's-level training prepares students to become administrators, planners, and practitioners.

On the doctoral level, some universities offer doctoral-level specializations with other academic and clinical departments. A few universities offer a Ph.D. in gerontology. Doctoral-level training prepares students for careers in teaching, research, administration, and clinical practice. Postdoctoral training programs or fellowships are available in gerontology and geriatrics. Many of these are funded through federal agencies and can be completed in clinical and academic settings.

The curricula of the gerontology majors, certificates, and minors vary with each school. Some programs are multidisciplinary in that they draw on the resources of a variety of academic disciplines (for example, Biology of Aging through the biology department, or Adult Development and Aging through the psychology department). Other programs are offered through a specific department, as in the case of a gerontological nursing certificate out of the nursing department. Also, though some colleges and universities emphasize academic theory and research, other colleges are more vocationally oriented. Still others have more of a liberal arts focus. The orientation of the gerontology program will be largely influenced by whether it is located within a school, department, academic center, or institute.

It should be noted that the term "certificate" is used to apply to both credit and noncredit gerontology programs. The noncredit certificate programs are usually conducted out of college and university centers for continuing education as nongraded professional development classes. More than one thousand schools offer course work and adult continuing education gerontology programs that address students' search for both personal and professional development. Gerontology associations, hospitals, training programs, and businesses can also offer them. Those enrolled may be individuals wishing to explore the gerontology field or gerontology practitioners seeking further knowledge. Students range from high school graduates to people with advanced degrees. They are usually granted continuing education units (CEUs), which are not college credits. In some professions, such as counseling, practitioners must obtain a minimum number of CEUs to maintain their professional status. Twelve hours of seminars cannot be equated with twelve to fifteen college-level courses; therefore, it is important in any job pursuit that the individual clarifies if his or her certificate was credit or noncredit.

Courses of Study

As discussed in this chapter, there are many educational options available for those who wish to work in gerontology or geriatrics. Colleges and universities have developed a multidisciplinary approach to gerontology training in the acknowledgment that most courses of study affect the quality of life for older adults. The following are representative of the academic departments offering gerontology courses:

Adult Education
Anthropology
Architecture/Environmental
   Design
Arts Therapies (Drama,
   Art, Dance, Music,
   Poetry, Photography)
Biology
Business Administration/
   Management
Communicative Disorders
Community Development

Community Health
Computer Science
Consumer Sciences
Counseling
Criminology
Demography
Dentistry
Economics
Education
Educational Psychology
Engineering
Exercise Physiology

Family Studies
Food Management
Governmental
 Administration
Health Administration
Health and Safety
 Education
Home Economics
Hospital and Health
 Administration
Human Ecology
Humanities
Interior Design
International Affairs
Labor Relations
Law
Library Sciences
Marketing
Media/Communications/
 Journalism
Medicine
Nursing
Nutrition
Occupational Therapy
Pharmacy

Philosophy
Physical Education
Physical Therapy
Policy/Research
 Administration
Political Science
Psychiatry
Psychology
Psychology/Clinical
 Psychology
Public Affairs/
 Administration
Public Health
Public Policy
Recreation/Leisure
Rehabilitation Counseling
Social Work/Human
 Services
Sociology
Special Education
Textiles
Theology
Urban Planning
Vocational and Career
 Education

Within each of these academic departments is one or more aging-related course, for example, Criminology—"Crime and the Elderly," Humanities—"The Art of Oral History," Recreation/ Leisure—"Leisure in Retirement."

The following is a sample list of courses that are offered in colleges and universities around the country. The diversity of the courses accentuates the fact that gerontology is a comprehensive, multidisciplinary field providing career opportunities in many professional areas.

Adult Development and Aging
Adult Education Processes
Adult Life Cycle
Advanced Gerontology Internship
Aging and the Contemporary Community
Aging and Human Development
Aging and Human Values
The Aging Individual in a Changing Society
Aging and Mental Health
Aging and Modernization
Aging and Society
Aging in Subcultures
Aging in Urban Societies
Aging in the Workforce
Biology of Aging
Children, Aging, Death and Dying—An Interdisciplinary Approach

The Church's Ministry with Older Adults
Communication and Aging
Community Environments for the Elderly
Community Planning for an Aging Population
Community Resources for the Aged
Coordinating Educational Programs for Older Adults in the Community
Counseling the Older Adult
Culture, Society, and Aging
Demography of Aging
Developing Models of Ministry with Older Adults
Developmental Psychology of Middle and Old Age
Disadvantaged Elderly
Dying, Death, and Bereavement
Economics of Aging

Education through the Life Span

Educational Programming for Older Adults

Elder Affairs in American Society

Eldercare Facilities

Elderly and the Family: Delivery of Services

Environmental Gerontology

Ethnicity in Aging

Faith and Understanding in Adulthood

Families across the Life Cycle

The Family in Later Life

Field Research in Gerontology

Food and Nutrition for the Elderly

Foundations of Aging—A Multidisciplinary View

Geography and the Elderly

Gerontological Social Work

Gerontology and the Helping Professions

Grandmothers, Mothers, and Daughters

Growing Old in America

The Handicapped Elderly

Health and Aging

High Tech for an Aging Society

Housing for the Elderly and Handicapped

Images of Aging in Literature

Individual and Group Work with the Elderly

Industrial Gerontology

Institutional and Noninstitutional Care of the Aged

The Institutionalized Elderly

Intellectual Development in the Aging Process

Interdisciplinary Methods of Teaching in Long-Term Care

Interdisciplinary Seminar in Life Span Development and Gerontology

Intergenerational Learning— Use of Senior Citizen Volunteers

Intergenerational Relationships

Internship in Gerontology

Interviewing and Assessment Skills with the Elderly

Issues and Applications in the Field of Aging

Issues and Perceptions of Aging

Issues in Minority Aging

Late Careers and Aging

Library and Information Services for Older Adults

Life Span and Community Education

Lifelong Learning

Literary and Sociological Aspects of Death

Loss and Grief

Meaningful Maturation for Elders

Myths and Realities of the Aging Process

Normal Aging

Old Age as Depicted in Literature

Older People and Organizations

The Older Person as an Adult Learner

The Older Woman

Organizational Health Care System

Philosophy of Aging

Potentialities of Aging

Problem Perspectives of Aging

Processes of Living and Dying

Professional Practice with Older People

Program Design and Adult Learning

Promoting Successful Aging

Psychobiology of Aging

Psychology of Adult Development

Psychology of Aging

Psychology of Maturity and Old Age

Psychology of Women—Life Span Approach

Psychosocial Aspects of Retirement

Race and Ethnicity in Aging

Reading for the Elderly

Recreation Programming for Older Adults

Religion and Aging

Research on Aging

Research in Cross-Cultural Aging

Retirement in American Society

Seminar in Adult
Socialization
Seminar on Chicano Aged
Seminar on Family
Gerontology
Seminar in Gerontology
Theory
Seminar on Memory Pro-
cesses in Aging
Skills for Serving the Frail
Elderly
Social Aspects of Aging
Social Gerontology
Social Policy and Programs
in Gerontology
Sociology of Aging
Sociology of Aging and
Retirement
Sociology of Aging in Rural
and Urban America
Sociology of Death and
Survivorship

Sociology of Life Stages
Special Problems of Aging
Blacks
Special Problems of the
Rural Elderly
Special Topics in Urban
Gerontology
Sport, Leisure, and Aging
Stress, Health, and Aging
Structuring the Environment
for the Elderly
Teaching Children about
Aging
Theology of Death, Suffer-
ing, Healing, and Afterlife
Theology and the Elderly
Theories of Age, Senility,
and Death in Literature
Thesis in Gerontology
Third World Aging
Values and Ethics in an
Aging Society

Every discipline offering academic gerontology training is rooted in a standard knowledge base. There are essential competencies encompassing study of the biological, psychological, and sociological aspects of aging. The core curriculum consists of courses in the sociology/social aspects of aging, psychology of aging or mental health aspects of aging, biology/physiology/health aspects of aging, health and human services programs and policies, gerontological research methods, and an internship or practicum. Further, a choice of gerontology electives enables the student to relate gerontological theory to individual career goals. For instance, Environment and Aging would be particularly appropriate for the architect, Counseling Older Adults for the social worker, Geriatric Nutrition for the dietitian. Electives in gerontology cover such topics as health care, housing, transportation, employment, retirement, and economics.

In selecting the course of study appropriate to one's career interest, the student should note that no one single discipline is the sole source of entry into a professional area. For instance, geriatric care managers may have degrees in psychology, social work, nursing, or other related fields. Also, so as not to limit their career scope, it is important that students fully appreciate the range of career possibilities within any single career area. For example, home economics incorporates such areas as apparel design (for example, adaptive clothing for physically challenged individuals), nutrition and dietetics, family studies (for example, caregiving and grandparenting), consumer education, and environmental design. Further, it is not sufficient to know only one's own professional area; to be effective, the gerontologist must be aware of all of the factors impacting on the quality of life of older adults. This holistic perspective has been promoted through the use of interdisciplinary teams in which gerontologists from various disciplines share their unique observations and recommendations to arrive at a comprehensive and accurate client needs assessment.

In choosing an academic gerontology program, the student needs to be sure that the college or university meets his or her individual needs. For instance, external degree/home study/distance education options may be particularly attractive to the individual who cannot or does not wish to learn via regular class attendance. Those interested in education through the computerized network should determine if the college or university has such distance education capabilities. Individuals wishing to have their prior volunteer or work experience in gerontology credited toward their degrees may be interested only in academic programs that permit some level of portfolio (life experience) review. Also, the ability to "test out" of courses by taking competency tests such as CLEP enables the student to receive academic credit for prior learning. One should determine if the college or university is accredited, as well as the individual department in which one is studying. If needed, the availability of scholarships and financial aid opportunities should be assessed.

The more comprehensive gerontology programs in higher education are frequently offered under the auspices of a college's or university's multidisciplinary institute on aging. These institutes on aging or centers on aging, as they are also called, promote interdepartmental teaching and research, develop interdisciplinary training sites, offer cross-listings of courses, establish field placements, and produce publications. These institutes are distinguished by their unique and innovative contributions to the gerontology field.

Since the gerontology field incorporates such a wide variety of occupations, as previously listed, it is not possible within the framework of this book to give background on the educational requirements and duties of each position. The appendixes in this book include contact information on professional associations for various career areas.

Positions in gerontology span all educational backgrounds from high school through postgraduate work. One's educational level will largely determine the responsibilities and income of a career in gerontology. This is illustrated, for example, by the levels of employment in gerontological nursing practice, which is a division within the American Nurses Association. For example, licensed practical nurses, or L.P.N.s, are required to study in a state-approved program for up to a year and pass a national licensing exam. The L.P.N. does not conduct any medical procedure independently but rather performs daily routine care under the supervision of a doctor or a registered nurse (R.N.). The R.N. with a bachelor's degree, on the other hand, is given additional responsibilities such as health education, counseling, and supervision. To become an R.N., one must graduate from an accredited school of nursing and pass a national licensure exam.

A geriatric nurse, or an R.N. with a specialization in gerontology, assumes responsibility for the elderly patient from initial needs assessment to discharge planning. Salaries for R.N.s are expected to rise as long-term care needs increase. The opportunity for advancement exists; homes for the aging promote R.N.s to positions as managers, directors of nursing, and staff development coordinators. The master's degree is required of the gerontological nurse specialist who performs less direct service and instead serves in the administrative capacity of researcher, consultant, teacher, and community organizer around issues of improving health care for the elderly.

Since the large numbers of older patients stretch the available resources of the R.N.s and L.P.N.s, geriatric aides or nursing assistants are hired to help with the bathing, feeding, and basic care of the patient. Nursing assistants in nursing homes are required to have completed seventy-five hours of training and pass a certifying exam. The training for geriatric aides extends anywhere from a few weeks to a year depending on the standards of the particular vocational school, high school, or college offering the training.

Internships/Practicums

Most major, minor, and certificate programs in gerontology require an internship (intensive field experience) in acknowledgment that the best learning is gained from "hands on" experience. Internships permit the future practitioners to test out classroom gerontological theory and personal skills in a laboratory situation under professional supervision. Some internships provide stipends; all provide academic credit.

Internship sites are as varied as gerontology careers themselves, ranging from hospices to mobile home parks, from adult day care centers to legal aid for the elderly programs. The student's academic advisor, who will have a list of sites of former interns as well as new potential sites, usually provides internship placement assistance. However, it should be noted that in such a broad and challenging career as gerontology, the student will often do best to initiate her or his own placement suited to individual goals. For instance, a political science major with a minor in gerontology may create an internship in a community affairs office in which he or she spearheads legislative advocacy on behalf of the elderly. By approaching an agency and offering to provide a new service, the student is demonstrating drive and commitment, qualities that incline the agency to view the candidate as a potential employee beyond the internship period.

The student can refer to numerous resources in selecting an internship site. The appendixes in this book list information on various gerontology and professional associations. Direct contact can be made with these organizations regarding internship application procedures. Also contained within the appendixes are bibliographical materials, which will be helpful in the internship development process.

Academic Gerontology Programs Extend to Community Service

In addition to undergraduate and graduate gerontology programs, most universities also conduct educational programs outside of the curriculum structure to make the information more accessible to the general community. These programs take the form of institutes, workshops, and summer school programs. The university also often serves the general community by making itself available as a resource to area agencies on aging. In that capacity, the university, through its division of continuing education and academic departments, offers the following services:

1. provision of technical assistance to individuals or groups serving older adults (for example, establishing a Friendly Visitors Program or designing a Blood Pressure Screening Project)
2. assistance in grants writing
3. survey of the community to determine direction that future curricula and community service projects should take
4. organization of conferences related to aging
5. application of academic research to the improved quality of life of older adults
6. offering of noncredit gerontology certificate programs
7. arrangement of professional development seminars

8. provision of gerontology community education programs (for example, caregiver training or pre-retirement counseling)
9. provision of publications and media resources to educate the public in gerontology
10. participation in legislative and advocacy forums on aging
11. establishment of a speakers' bureau to publicly address issues on aging

An exciting illustration of this cooperative programming between academia and the community is the concept of the teaching nursing home in gerontological nursing. In this capacity, the gerontology faculty is hired jointly by a nursing school and a nursing home. The education of the nursing students is enriched by the fact that they are directly involved in real life situations in the nursing home. The nursing faculty is able to use the nursing home as a laboratory for research in long-term care. Since the faculty is involved with the nursing home staff's in-service teaching as part of the teaching nursing home concept, they are able to keep abreast of the most current developments in the field, which in turn enhances their teaching in the classroom with nursing students.

In the provision of training to health care professionals, a number of centers of higher education have been designated as Geriatric Education Centers (GECs) federally funded through the Bureau of Health Professions. In 2000, thirty-four Geriatric Education Centers were awarded a total of $7.4 million. Interdisciplinary in philosophy and practice, GECs involve one or more schools of medicine and one or more of the following departments: nursing, pharmacy, dentistry, public health, podiatry, optometry, allied health, health education, health sciences administration, physician assistance, and social work. Their functions include technical assistance; continuing education; staff in-service training; information dissemination; grants writing; consultation; geriatric residencies, traineeships, and fellowships; curriculum development; and clinical geriatrics training. Health care professionals making use of GEC services come from such settings as ambulatory care clinics, community hospitals, nursing homes, rehabilitation centers, home health agencies, Area Agencies on Aging, and senior citizen centers. Many of them attend as a requirement to maintain their professional credential within their respective professional association (for example, the American Nursing Association or the American Occupational Therapy Association).

5

TRENDS IMPACTING
AGING SERVICES

THIS CHAPTER WILL discuss some of the major societal factors that all gerontologists need to consider in providing services to older adults.

Grandparenting

Society associates grandparenting with rewarding, anticipated, intergenerational relationships. Though it is true that most older adults look forward to grandparenting and ultimately relish the time that they spend with their grandchildren, for many grandparents, the profile of grandparenthood is fraught with unexpected, excessive demands. These grandparents, primarily grandmothers, are literally raising their grandchildren due to the absence or ineffectiveness of their real parents.

In America there are 633,000 grandparents sixty-five and older who raise grandchildren in their households. The number of three-generation households has increased. Some minority elders, particularly those recently immigrating to this society, find that they are virtual isolates, remaining in the home with grandchildren while the grandchildren's parents are elsewhere.

Older adults are particularly subject to physical and emotional stress due to the demands of parenting. The period of their lives that they believed they could devote to leisure is now consumed by parenting duties that they thought they had left far behind. Many are forced to quit jobs and sever social contacts. There is natural frustration and anger at being in this situation at this stage of their lives. The causes for the grandparent becoming the parent are many: her or his child—the parent—may be deceased, divorced, incarcerated, mentally ill, a substance abuser, an AIDS victim, or may have abandoned the child. The problems these grandparents experience in raising children have led many to seek support groups such as Grandparents as Parents (GAP) for resource information and emotional nurturing.

The median national income of grandparents raising grandchildren is approximately $18,000, half that of a traditional family. It is difficult to make ends meet. The current system of funding foster parents, but not grandparents as parents, actually favors the foster care system and works against grandparents keeping their families together.

In addition to seeking legal assistance pertaining to their new parenting responsibilities, many grandparents have also gone to court to challenge grandchild visitation restrictions established during parents' divorce proceedings. Gerontologists interested in advocacy and legislative work are needed to advance grandparents' rights. Social service workers will increasingly be called on to provide resources and support to the growing ranks of parenting grandparents.

Ethics

As people live longer, they, their caregivers, and service providers are in a greater position of exercising choice regarding the quality of their later lives. The Patient Self-Determination Act (PSDA) of 1991 gave terminally ill patients in hospitals, nursing homes, and home-care settings the right to make their own health care decisions. Further, community education on advanced directives (such as living wills, health care proxy, and durable power of attorney) is familiarizing the public with the importance of recording their health care wishes in anticipation of illness or mental incapacity. In the living will, the individual indicates which life-sustaining measures he or she would find acceptable or unacceptable (for example, hydration, ventilation, nutrition) in the event of a terminal condition creating mental incapacity. A durable power of attorney or health care proxy is a designation of someone to make health care decisions on the individual's behalf in the event that he or she becomes mentally incapacitated.

Aging in a society of medical technology has resulted in serious questions regarding the duration and quality of life. Technology has given us the ability to extend life, and with this capability comes added moral responsibility. The ethical questions to be addressed include: end-of-life decisions including euthanasia, potential rationing of high-tech medical services, use of psychotropic medication, biomedical research termed "anti-aging interventions," and utilization of life-extending technology.

To grapple with these concerns, ethics teams or committees have formed in health care settings. These groups deal with questions of law, medicine, psychology, morality, and religion. The teams consist of such individuals as medical staff, social workers, clergy, lawyers, institutional representatives, patients, and their caregivers. They engage in staff and community education and make policy recommendations on individual medical cases. Most of the nation's hospitals have ethics committees, while few nursing homes do. There will be a growth in the existence of these interdisciplinary teams, for society is acknowledging that the potential and usage of complex medical technology demands ethical, rational decision making. Gerontologists from various disciplines will continue to assume critically important roles in these ethics committees.

Intergenerational Programming

Gerontologists are involved in developing and conducting a variety of intergenerational programs. There has been increased recognition of the fact that age-segregated activities are not necessarily conducive to the total well-being of older adults. In fact, increasingly, the interdependence between youth and elders is acknowledged for its importance. Gerontologists are developing programs that bring older adults and youth together for diverse educational and recreational experiences.

Though the term "intergenerational" usually connotes images of older adults caring for preschoolers, it actually refers to any interrelationship among people of different generations; so, in the case of aging services, intergenerational relationships consist of interpersonal communication between elders and infants, children, teens, young adults, and middle adults.

In intergenerational programs, generations may share resources, as when youth and elders cooperatively volunteer at a food bank for the needy. In other cases, the elders may view themselves as being the primary givers of service, for instance, when retired professionals counsel young people beginning their careers. In other intergenerational programs, elders are considered the primary recipients of service, for example, when 4-H members provide chore assistance for elderly home owners who may be frail and economically needy.

The prevalence of multigenerational families living together is declining due to mobility and emotionally fractured families, so the presence of grandparents is often lacking. Therefore, there is an even stronger need in society for organized intergenerational programming.

In intergenerational programs, there is no one giver or receiver, for both generations reap the rewards of intergenerational exchange. Interaction with older adults provides youth and adults with invaluable role models of aging. Without such interaction, youth would grow up with only negative societal stereotypes as their frame of reference. For elders, the interaction with other generations enables them to experience the satisfaction of "passing on" their knowledge and values. This "elder function" has been identified as being crucial to our well-being and positive self-image in later life. There is considerable satisfaction and inner peace derived from sharing one's personal heritage and knowing it will be preserved after one dies. For youth, there is real value in interacting with elders who share their wisdom and inspiration. Older adults, in turn, benefit from the new insights of youth.

Consequently, it is no longer assumed that a service will be more effective if provided in age-segregated settings. There will be increased emphasis in gerontology studies on life span development, so as to provide a broader framework for intergenerational programs. For instance, the Association for Gerontology in Higher Education and Generations Together of the University of Pittsburgh received a three-year grant from the National Corporation for Service Learning to offer students at thirty campuses the opportunity to engage in intergenerational service learning projects. Those working in youth and aging services continue to form coalitions to foster collaborative services. For instance, intergenerational day care settings are recognized as being therapeutic and stimulating to both youth and elders alike. Gerontologists from all disciplines will be involved in determining how their professional areas, such as education, housing, recreation, and social services, can better serve older adults through age-integrated approaches.

Older Women

Women continue to have longer life spans than men do. However, it is not solely because they live longer that women experience greater obstacles in later life; it is the cumulative effects of sexism and economic inequity that largely result in their later life struggles.

Though women comprise the majority of older adults worldwide, particularly in the over-seventy-five age group, there has been inadequate attention to their lifestyle needs. Many older women have insufficient economic resources, inferior health care, and inadequate housing. Although it is true that increasing numbers of older women are entering the workforce for the first time or as a second career, they usually find their living expenses and caregiving costs outweighing any benefits from their earnings. Chronic illness such as diabetes and arthritis affects many older adults, who, as they age, require more assistance. As women live longer, they increasingly will need to draw on the services of health care agencies. Half of women over seventy-five live alone and two-thirds are widowed. Since many older women are single and child-less, they cannot call on informal caregivers for assistance; therefore, there is increased demand for more formal caregivers in the social services network. Gerontology careers will expand in response to this growing need.

The challenges of aging are particularly acute among older women. The number of women over eighty-five will continue to grow in large numbers. Most elderly poor are women. Minority older females are particularly caught in this cycle of poverty. Recent studies revealed that while 19 percent of white older women who lived alone were in poverty, the figure rose to 50 percent among older Black and Latino women. On average, elderly women's incomes are more than one-third less than those of elderly men. Working women's pensions are less than those of men are. Even if women have worked the same jobs as men, they have been paid an unequal wage. Women's domestic roles are unpaid and thus have not been counted as an earnings base for pension determination. Social Security inequities favor the husband's earnings over any wages the wife may have earned.

Older women are the primary caregivers for their spouses and families. About 25 percent of women over age seventy have no living children and thus have limited assistance with caregiving. Spousal impoverishment often results from the cost of caring for an ailing husband. It is not uncommon for an older woman to be caring for both children and their parents. It is increasingly likely that those sixty-five and over will care for at least one parent. Disabled adults are frequently cared for by their aging mothers.

Grandmothers are the ones most often called on to care for grand-children caught in some family dysfunction.

Health problems of women in later life reflect the need for more health education and research on women's health related to such issues as breast cancer, menopause, urinary incontinence, and osteoporosis. Though osteoporosis occurs in males, it is largely evident in women. Currently one out of every six American women will develop osteoporosis. One in two women over sixty-five will develop fractures due to the condition. An estimated eighty thousand women will die annually from complications associated with hip fractures.

Despite the fact that women comprise the majority of the older population, gerontological research and services have not been sufficiently directed toward their unique needs. Older women will continue to be the prime consumers of services; therefore, members of the gerontology profession are encouraged to devote more attention to their needs.

Minority Elderly

Anyone planning to work as a gerontologist needs to be knowledgeable in the cultural and ethnic backgrounds of the older persons with whom they work. Since most of the gerontology research has been written from a white, Euro-American perspective, there has been insufficient attention to the backgrounds and needs of all racial groups. We live in a pluralistic society, and there is a great need for multicultural awareness to acquaint gerontologists with the diverse ethnic backgrounds of the elderly in this country.

Minority groups are defined as those ethnic groups receiving unequal allocation of this nation's resources. These minority groups, such as Latino, Native American, African American, and Asian American, while increasing in number in this country, nevertheless, continue to receive limited services. In 1985 minority elderly in the United States represented 14 percent of America's older population; by 2050, they will have risen to 33 percent. The U.S. Census Bureau states that there will be more than 3 million Latino elders in 2015 and 6.7 million in 2040. The Latino population is the fastest growing minority population in the United States. The African American population, according to the U.S. Census, will rise from 4.5 million in 2015 to 8.7 million in 2040. Thus, we can anticipate that Latino elderly and African American elderly will comprise an increasing majority of the elderly population. The Census Bureau projects that by 2050, 16 percent of the older population in the United States will be Latino, 12 percent will be non-Hispanic Black, and 7 percent will be non-Hispanic Asian and Pacific Islanders.

Minority elderly, compared to white elderly, fare worse in such lifestyle factors as longevity, health, housing, education, employment, and income. For example, Native American elderly have an unemployment rate of approximately 80 percent and a poverty rate of 61 percent. The higher mortality rate of minority elders reflects the toll taken on lives that have struggled against lifetimes of discrimination and public neglect. For instance, the term "triple jeopardy" has been coined to describe the multiple life threats of being an elderly, African American female in America—ageism, racism, and sexism. Those minority elders who are non-English speaking are said to experience a fourth jeopardy to their survival—the language barrier.

Primary to working effectively with minority elderly is an understanding of their identities; all too often an ethnic group is given a label that disregards its unique components. For instance, Native

Americans prefer to be called by their individual tribal names (for example, Navajo or Cherokee) and not as Native Americans. There are over five hundred North American tribes who speak more than two hundred different languages. The Latino population also consists of a diversity of cultural backgrounds that need to be acknowledged. Therefore, one would not refer to an individual as Hispanic, but rather as Puerto Rican, Mexican, Cuban, and so forth. Similarly, Asian Americans comprise many groups including Chinese, Filipino, Asian Indian, Japanese, Korean, Vietnamese, and Pacific-Islanders including Guamanians, Hawaiians, and Samoans.

Despite the fact that the number of minority elderly continues to increase at a rate higher than that of white elderly, services to minority elderly have not been at all comparable to the need. There are many reasons why existing aging services have not adequately met the needs of minority elderly. The lack of bilingual staff and educational materials has prevented many minority elderly from obtaining information on existing services. Also, many aging services are located in areas that are not accessible to minority elderly. The lack of transportation, community outreach workers, or satellite programs isolate the minority elderly from services. Further, many minority elderly and their families are suspicious of availing themselves of organized aging services because their past mistreatment has led them to be mistrustful of society. Discrimination over years has resulted in social alienation and, thus, disconnection from community services.

Another obstacle is the fact that many gerontologists falsely assume that minority elderly are served by tightly knit family units, and thus do not need social services. Gerontologists often adopt the stereotypical view that minority elders consider organized aging services as an insult or threat and prefer to rely solely on family for support. Though it is true that some cultures have high levels of family support, it is invalid for gerontologists to conclude that their own assistance should not be offered. It is because some gerontologists have kept such a distance from many ethnic groups that the problems of these minority elderly have continued to accelerate. As these families become diffused due to family mobility, economic pressure, and societal influences, it becomes increasingly difficult for them to rely solely on family members to fulfill caregiving needs of the elderly. Therefore, the needs for organized aging services do exist and will continue to grow.

To improve their level of services to minority elderly, gerontologists must move away from an ethnocentric perspective, which ignores the richness of other cultures. They need to understand the unique cultural influences impacting on their clients; these influences would include, for example, historical experiences, values, religious practices, family relationships, forms of verbal and nonverbal communication, and attitudes towards utilizing aging services. A minority elder's present attitude toward life in America will be largely influenced by the amount of time he or she has lived in America and whether he or she was born here, immigrated here at a younger age, or immigrated recently. If the elder is a recent immigrant, he or she may experience particular grief at loss of the homeland and may feel adrift and devalued in American society where roles for elders do not correlate with the roles assumed in the homeland. This loss of status may result in physical and mental health problems. If the elder is non-English speaking and must rely on friends and family, he or she may feel a sense of shame in having to ask grandchildren to read and explain information. Some may find the American diet harmful to their systems. Since many have not had the opportunity to build a pension through a lifetime of earnings in this country, economic deprivation is widespread. Many have experienced some form of torture and trauma in their homeland and now live daily with those emotional and physical scars. A terminally ill elder may reject hospital care and wish to return to the homeland because his or her tradition indicates that unless one is buried in one's native soil, one's soul will never be at rest. A representative from another ethnic group may reject a health care worker because he or she subscribes to folk healing.

Opportunities need to be made available for minority elders to share their skills. For instance, Native American elders could teach their craftsmanship to younger generations. Ethnic festivals permit elders to share their traditions and folklore with the general community. Also, greater attention needs to be given to the recruitment of minority elders to serve as trainers and outreach workers. Minority elders are frequently more open to availing themselves of aging services if they are offered by their peers.

Minority students are encouraged to enter the gerontology field. Services to minority elders need to operate from within their communities rather than from outside of them. For instance, if elders frequent a particular religious institution, then this can serve as the hub for social services and mobile geriatric outreach services.

Any gerontologist, whether a home health aide, elder law attorney, or any other practitioner, will be interacting with elders from a variety of ethnic backgrounds. To avoid unnecessary clashes or misinterpretations and to ensure qualitative services, multicultural education of gerontologists is essential. Minority members, young and old, should be actively involved in the design and instruction of this training. This sensitization will help ensure that gerontologists are aware of the various needs of the minority elders in the community, and thus respond with relevant, accessible services.

6

A Promising Future

It is important that the gerontology career one selects reflects one's skills and interests. Future gerontologists are encouraged to engage in many fieldwork and volunteer experiences in a variety of gerontological settings so as to learn which roles bring the greatest satisfaction and joy. Many people enter the gerontology field as a second career; such individuals should explore how enjoyable aspects of their prior careers could be applied to gerontology. For instance, a former professor may draw on her or his teaching background to direct an intergenerational arts program or to teach older adults a series of health/wellness seminars.

Gerontologists as Entrepreneurs

A job hunt should not solely revolve around reviewing the classified ads. These ads do not represent the extent of career opportunities; those advertisers that identify themselves as aging services usually only refer to health care positions. Career seekers should adopt a proactive, creative approach. This is referred to as "entrepreneurship": the exercise of initiative and creativity in determining how one's professional skills can be directed to the service of older adults. For example, a business major/gerontology minor graduate may approach a bank manager and offer to create and perform the duties of a senior services specialist. In convincing the manager that the position is necessary due to the rising number of elder customers and their extensive banking needs (for example, pensions, investments), the gerontologist is being entrepreneurial. One can also be entrepreneurial by creating a central focus on aging services within one's existing job. For example, a commercial travel agent who specializes in intergenerational travel options for elders is demonstrating entrepreneurship in gerontology.

Entrepreneurs in gerontology are advised to develop a business plan. For instance, someone interested in administering a for-profit chore assistance service for elders would need to obtain the following information in the business plan:

1. What is the community's need for the chore assistance service? What were the results of the needs assessment?
2. Do the demographic variables of the elderly (age, health, family support, and socioeconomic status) indicate that they need and can afford the chore assistance service?
3. Is there competition from any other service provider?
4. Are there possibilities of partnerships with any other individuals or agencies?
5. What are the philosophy/goals/objectives/policies and procedures governing your service?
6. What marketing strategies will you use?

7. As the administrator of the program, do you see any need for further training (for example, accounting, interviewing skills, marketing)?
8. What is the necessary initial outlay of funding? What is the projected income?
9. According to what timeline do you anticipate completing your business plan objectives?
10. What is your long-term forecasting for the future? How will you maintain and develop your long-range plans?
11. What are your personal career assets: networking contacts, reference letters, certificates, awards, commendations?

Occupational Outlook Quarterly indicated that at least 13 percent of the labor force was self-employed. These jobs included such areas as business management, consulting services, entertainment and recreation, personal services, and professional services (law, architecture, and medicine). Gerontologists work within all of these areas with older adults as their primary consumers. There is great employment opportunity in the gerontology field due to the diversity of the older adult population and the diversity of the career areas serving these elders. Entrepreneurship enables the individual to maximize his or her career potential in gerontology.

Salaries

Since careers in gerontology cross over many professional areas and represent all levels of required skills and educational backgrounds, there can be no one representative salary range. For instance, the administrator and van driver of a nursing home are each employed in a gerontology career but represent very different ends of the pay scale. Also, within a single occupation, there will be variations of salary level. For instance, two social workers may have the same educational background, but the social worker in the Medicaid-funded nursing home will usually make less than the social worker employed as an eldercare counselor in a profit-making corporation.

The diversity of employment opportunities in gerontology does not permit inclusion of all possible salaries in this text. Gerontology is a broad field encompassing any career in which older adults are the sole or major focus. This limitless range means that there is no single comprehensive listing of all possible gerontology careers and their corresponding salaries.

Because one's salary is determined by the setting in which one works and the extent of one's entrepreneurship, no standard salary levels exist in the gerontology field. Within each occupation there will be a variance in salary dependent on a number of factors, such as educational background, prior experience, and geographical area. For more comprehensive salary range information on a gerontology career of your interest, consult the professional association for that career, for example, the National Association of Social Workers, the National Association for Drama Therapy, or the American Dietetic Association.

Becoming a Gerontologist

As diverse as the field itself are the ways by which gerontologists establish their careers. There are many different methods to choose from in becoming a gerontologist. Each career pathway is a personal venture of initiative and creativity.

The future gerontologist is encouraged to become an active member of gerontological organizations locally, statewide, and nationally (for example, the National Council on Aging). In addition to keeping one current in gerontology, the professional affiliation also fosters networking, field work, and internship opportunities that often lead to employment. Many times, scholarships and fellowships are available. Attendance at organizational conferences enables the member to remain current with the fast-changing conditions impacting on older adults and aging services. The material presented in these conference workshops reflects the current state of affairs in the gerontology field. Conference workshop topics serve to give the gerontology job seeker some invaluable job growth indicators. Also, many of today's gerontology associations have job bank listings at their conferences. The professional journals received as part of organizational membership also provide significant information on gerontology career opportunities. The appendixes in this book contain contact information on national and international gerontology associations.

Gerontology job announcements can be obtained from a variety of sources, including governmental agencies, professional associations, and educational institutions. Many professional associations have job bank lists and links to other employment opportunities. There are professional associations for each career area (for example, the National Association for Social Workers), many of which have membership subsections on gerontology.

A number of important publications serve as gerontology career references. The *Encyclopedia of Associations* is an annual multivolume publication listing trade associations, professional societies, labor unions, and fraternal and civic organizations. Key employment publications are the *Occupational Outlook Handbook, Occupational Outlook Quarterly, Guide to American Directories, Directory of Directories*, and the *Directory of Counseling Services*, a publication of the International Association of Counselors (IAC).

Also, annual reports of gerontology agencies and foundations reveal the growth areas in aging services. Job prospects can also be obtained by reviewing chamber of commerce directories, telephone yellow pages, and job postings in libraries. The appendixes in this text contain resource information on websites and publications addressing gerontology career exploration.

The job-seeking gerontologist should explore many key employment resources. For one, each state's Department of Employment offers consultation workshops and job placement assistance. The Department of Veterans Affairs offers job postings and stipends. Anyone interested in civil service positions should contact the Regional Office of the Civil Service Commission. Job leads can also be obtained from governmental Area Agencies on Aging. State Units on Aging can be contacted for a list of agencies and organizations.

Career information and counseling are available from a variety of sources including public libraries, high school guidance departments, college career planning and placement offices, vocational rehabilitation agencies, community counseling services, state employment services offices, and private counseling services. In a library search, one should look at computer listings under "careers" and "vocations," and under specific fields. Trade and professional magazines about specific occupations and industries provide sources of employment leads. Schools often provide employment assistance in the form of career days, guest speakers, field trips, and individual counseling and testing. Career counselors assist in the job seeking process in a variety of ways, including the administration of interest inventories and aptitude tests.

The Internet has become an increasingly invaluable source of career information. Due to the growth of online listings, there are many gerontology job leads available on the World Wide Web.

Most professional associations, academic institutions, government agencies, and companies maintain Internet sites that include such information as latest accomplishments, future activities, links to career resources, educational opportunities, and job openings. The U.S. Department of Labor lists job openings through America's Job Bank (ajb.dni.us). Federal government jobs are available from the Office of Personnel Management (usajobs.opm.gov). Information on apprenticeships is available from the U.S. Department of Labor's Bureau of Apprenticeship and Training (doleta.gov/indi vid/apprent.htm).

Future gerontologists are advised to talk to those already working in the gerontology field regarding such areas as training, responsibilities, and career advancement potential. Also, future gerontologists are encouraged to assume part-time jobs and volunteer roles to obtain more "hands-on" experiences in the field. In many cases, these experiences can be developed into full-time positions.

The titles "gerontologist" and "geriatrician" are not terms commonly used in society when naming work with older adults. Instead jobs will be described in such language as a "nurse working with the elderly" or a "recreation director in an adult care community." Therefore, the job seeker looking through the classified ads should realize that jobs in gerontology will not be listed as such, but will be found under the career area itself (for example, recreation, education, or social services).

Gerontologists as Visionaries for the Future

Essential to any gerontology career planning is an understanding of societal trends and the gerontology career projections they point to. This text has examined the many conditions impacting on older adults, some of which include increased longevity, health care demands, economic inequity, work and retirement issues, housing needs, the changing family, multiculturalism, legal concerns, and the influence of technology. In response to this information, future gerontologists should be able to project where services need to be developed and, thus, prepare for gerontology careers providing those services.

We live in a world that does not acknowledge that our most pressing problems affect older adults as much, if not more, than the overall population. When the term "at risk" is used, it is usually in reference to youth characterized by such problems as substance abuse, AIDS, illiteracy, and suicide. However, the term "at risk" also should be used for many older adults who are experiencing the aforementioned problems and many more.

Despite the burgeoning older adult population, awareness of gerontology as a field of study and employment is still relatively new. The central challenge of the gerontology field is to recognize the diverse lifestyles of the older population and to create services appropriate to those varied and unique individuals. Gerontologists must recognize that services should be individually tailored to the needs of all elders, well and frail, rich and poor, male and female, white and minority, urban and rural. Thus, one gerontologist may be engaged in marketing consumer products to older adults with extensive discretionary income, while another gerontologist may be working to find employment for low-income retirees. One gerontologist may be assisting a couple in locating a retirement condominium, while another gerontologist is busy designing adaptive equipment to enable a disabled widow to remain in her single-room occupancy unit.

The older adult population, characterized by an increasing diversity of lifestyles and complexities of needs, calls for a varied workforce of resourceful gerontologists. Today's gerontologists are in an exciting position to become active visionaries as each, in his or her own unique way, blends talents, training, caring, and conviction in working for an enriched quality of life for older adults.

Appendix A

Federal Agencies Related to Aging Services

For more information on federal agencies, contact the following agencies and organizations at the addresses provided. To locate your state's agencies related to aging services, go to aoa.dhhs.gov/agingsites/state.html.

Administration on Aging (AOA)
330 Independence Ave. SW
Washington, DC 20201
aoa.dhhs.gov

Bureau of Health Professions
Health Resources and Services Administration
5600 Fishers La., Rm. 8-103
Rockville, MD 20857
hrsa.dhhs.gov/bhpr

Centers for Disease Control and Prevention
4770 Buford Hwy. NE
Atlanta, GA 30341
cdc.gov

Centers for Medicare & Medicaid Services (formerly HCFA)
7500 Security Blvd.
Baltimore, MD 21244
http://cms.hhs.gov

Corporation for National and Community Service
1201 New York Ave. NW, 9th Fl.
Washington, DC 20525
cns.gov

Formerly ACTION, it supervises the Retired Senior Volunteer Program, Foster Grandparent Program, and Senior Companion Program, which place senior volunteers with families and agencies needing assistance. Also oversees SCORE, Senior Corps of Retired Executives, in which senior volunteers provide business/technical assistance to the community.

Department of Education
400 Maryland Ave. SW
Washington, DC 20202
ed.gov

Department of Housing and Urban Development (HUD)
451 Seventh St. SW
Washington, DC 20515
hud.gov

Department of Labor
200 Constitution Ave. NW
Washington, DC 20210
dol.gov

The Department of Labor includes the Bureau of Apprenticeship and Training, Pension and Welfare Benefit Administration, Women's Bureau National Resource and Information Center, and Senior Community Service Employment Program (part-time employment program for low-income seniors fifty-five years and older).

Department of Veteran's Affairs
Office of Public Affairs
810 Vermont Ave. NW
Washington, DC 20420
va.gov

Equal Employment Opportunity Commission
1801 L St. NW
Washington, DC 20507
eeoc.gov

Federal Council on the Aging
Rm. 4280, HHS-N330
Independence Ave. SW
Washington, DC 20201

Federal Interagency Forum on Aging-Related Statistics
6525 Belcrest Rd., Rm. 790
Hyattsville, MD 20782
agingstats.gov

Member agencies include: Administration on Aging, Agency for Healthcare Research and Quality, Bureau of Labor Statistics, U.S. Census Bureau,

Centers for Medicare and Medicaid Services (HCFA), Department of Veteran's Affairs, National Center for Health Statistics, National Institute on Aging, Office of the Assistant Secretary for Planning and Evaluation (Health and Human Services), Office of Management and Budget, and Social Security Administration.

Food and Nutrition Information Center
U.S. Department of Agriculture
National Agricultural Library Bldg.
Rm. 304
Beltsville, MD 20705
nal.usda.gov/fnic

National Association of Area Agencies on Aging
927 Fifteenth St., 6th Fl.
Washington, DC 20005
n4a.org

National Association of County Aging Programs
440 First St. NW
Washington, DC 20001

National Association of State Units on Aging
1225 Eye St. NW, Ste. 725
Washington, DC 20005
nasua.org

National Center for Health Statistics
   (part of Centers for Disease Control)
6525 Belcrest Rd.
Hyattsville, MD 20782
cdc.gov/nchs

National Clearinghouse for Primary Care Information
8201 Greensboro Dr., Ste. 600
McLean, VA 22 101
bphc.hrsa.gov

National Institute on Aging
National Institutes of Health
Bldg. 31, Rm. 5C27
31 Center Dr., MSC 2292
Bethesda, MD 20892
nia.nih.gov

Part of the National Institutes of Health, NIA is the federal government's principal agency concerned with the health interests of older adults and the support of biomedical, social, and behavioral research related to aging processes. Publishes *Age Page*, fact sheets on aging. NIA has established eleven centers on the Demography of Aging to provide innovative and policy-relevant research on such issues as health, social factors, and economics. NIH also oversees the National Women's Health Information Center, National Institute on Drug Abuse, National Institute on Alcohol Abuse and Alcoholism, National Institute of Nursing Research, and National Institute of Mental Health.

National Institute on Aging Information Center
P.O. Box 8057
Gaithersburg, MD 20898

National Institute on Alcohol Abuse and Alcoholism
National Institute on Drug Abuse
200 Independence Ave. SW
Washington, DC 20201
niaaa.nih.gov

National Institute of Education
555 New Jersey Ave. NW
Washington, DC 20201
nie.edu.sg

National Institute of Mental Health
5600 Fishers La., Rm. 15C-05
Rockville, MD 20857
nimh.nih.gov

Part of the federal government's Alcohol, Drug Abuse, and Mental Health Administration, NIMH supports research in the causes, prevention, and treatment of mental and emotional illnesses. NIMH's Mental Disorders of the Aging Program researches the interrelationship between aging and mental health.

National Library Service
Library of Congress
Washington, DC 20542
loc.gov/nls

Office of Disease Prevention and Health Promotion
Mary Switzer Bldg., Rm. 2132
330 C St. SW
Washington, DC 20201
http://odphp.osophs.dhhs.gov

Public Health Service
Health and Human Services Department (HHS)
200 Independence Ave. SW
Washington, DC 20201
http://phs.os.dhhs.gov/ophs/default.htm

Small Business Administration
409 Third St. SW, Ste. 4200
Washington, DC 20416
sba.gov

Social Security Administration
6401 Security Blvd., Rm. 4300
Baltimore, MD 21235
ssa.gov

State Department Employment Information Office
(Civil Service Positions)
Twenty-second and D Streets
Washington, DC 20520

Substance Abuse and Mental Health Services Administration
Department of Health and Human Services
5600 Fishers La.
Rockville, MD 20857
samhsa.gov

U.S. Bureau of the Census
Population Division
Washington, DC 20233

Regional and National Associations in Gerontology

CONTACT THE FOLLOWING organizations for more information.

Regional

Hawaii-Pacific Gerontological Society
P.O. Box 3714
Honolulu, HI 96812
hpgs.org

Midwest Council for Social Research in Aging
University of Minnesota
Sociology Dept.
Minneapolis, MN 55455

New England Gerontological Society
1 Cutts Rd.
Durham, NH 03824

Northeastern Gerontological Society
4 Country Club Dr.
West Simsbury, CT 06117

Southern Gerontological Society
1110 Thomasville Rd., Ste. 110
Tallahassee, FL 32303
wfu.edu/academic-departments/gerontology/sgs

Southwest Society on Aging
North Texas State University
P.O. Box 13346
Denton, TX 76203
swsaging.org/swsa

National

Aging in America
1500 Pelham Pkwy. S
Bronx, NY 10461
Research and service organization for gerontology professionals. Conducts research projects, gives educational and training seminars, and designs in-service curricula for long-term and acute care facilities. Conducts Projects with Industry program that helps elderly enter into the workforce. Provides programs to New York City older adults. Maintains speaker's bureau.

American Association of Retired Persons (AARP)
601 E St. NW
Washington, DC 20049
aarp.org

Serves the needs and interests of older adults through legislative advocacy, research, informational publications and audiovisual materials, and community education programs. Sponsors community service programs in crime prevention, tax aid, and defensive driving. AARP membership benefits include pre-retirement planning assistance and discounts on pharmaceuticals, travel, and insurance. Publishes *Modern Maturity* magazine, *Working Age*, and *Bulletin*. Legal Counseling for the Elderly is an affiliate.

American Geriatric Society
350 Fifth Ave.
New York, NY 10018
americangeriatrics.org

Promotes geriatric education and research. Provides leadership to health care professionals, policy makers, and the public by developing, implementing, and advocating programs in patient care, research, professional and public education, and public policy. Publishes *Directory of Fellowship Training Programs in Geriatric Medicine* in the United States and Canada, *Journal of the American Geriatric Society*, and *American Geriatrics Society Newsletter*. Posts jobs.

American Society on Aging
833 Market St., Ste. 511
San Francisco, CA 94103
asaging.org

Works to enhance the well-being of older individuals and to foster unity among those working with and for the elderly. Offers twenty-five continuing education programs for professionals in aging-related fields. Sponsors forums and networks in the following areas: spirituality, older adult education, mental health, lesbian and gay aging issues, business, technology, pre-retirement planning, multicultural aging, managed care, and aging, disability, and rehabilitation. Offers member affiliates in these areas. Publishes *Aging Today* and *Generations*. Provides an ASA Job Board. ASA Student Section lists conference opportunities and research awards.

Association for Gerontology in Higher Education
1001 Connecticut Ave., Ste. 410
Washington, DC 20005
aghe.org

Promotes gerontology in higher education through research, publications, technical assistance, and advocacy. Publications include the quarterly newsletter *AGHExchange*, gerontology bibliographies, and articles on education and employment in gerontology. Publishes the *National Directory of Educational Programs in Gerontology and Geriatrics*, a directory of academic programs nationwide. Additional publications include: *Standards and Guidelines for Gerontology Programs*, *Determining the Impact of Gerontology Preparation on Personnel in the Aging Network*, and *Diversity and Change in Gerontology, Geriatrics, and Aging Studies Programs in Institutes of Higher Education*. Provides sample syllabi, directory of schools, and text on guidelines for programs.

Gerontological Society of America
1030 Fifteenth St. NW, Ste. 250
Washington, DC 20005
geron.org

Promotes scientific study of aging, gerontology training, and the development of public policy reflecting gerontological research. Publishes *The Gerontologist*, *Gerontology News*, and the *Journals of Gerontology* incorporating four areas: biological sciences, medical sciences, psychological sciences, and sociological sciences.

National Council on the Aging
409 Third St., SW
Washington, DC 20024
ncoa.org

Committed to policy making, advocacy, and the development of model programs, education, and standards. Includes the National Institute on Community-Based Long-Term Care (NICLC), National Adult Day Services Association, National Institute on Senior Housing (NISH), National Center on Rural Aging (NCRA), National Institute of Senior Centers (NISC), National Association of Older Worker Employment Services (NAOWES), Health Promotion Institute (HPI), National Center for Voluntary Leadership in Aging (NCVLA), National Institute on Financial Issues and Services for Elders (NIFISE), and National Interfaith Coalition on Aging (NICA). NCOA's Family Friends program links senior volunteers with families in need due to poverty, homelessness, AIDS, and children's chronic illness or disability. Publishes *Innovations in Aging* and *Abstracts in Social Gerontology*.

APPENDIX C

Associations for Professionals Involved in Aging Services

THIS LIST OF professional associations includes a sampling of many areas of employment related to gerontology/geriatrics. If a career in which you are interested does not appear here, refer to the *Encyclopedia of Associations*.

Accrediting Commission on Education for Health Services
    Administration
730 Eleventh St. NW
Washington, DC 20001
acehsa.org

American Academy of Physical Medicine and Rehabilitation
IBM Plaza, Ste. 2500
Chicago, IL 60603
aapmr.org

American Academy of Physician Assistants
950 N. Washington St.
Alexandria, VA 22314
aapa.org

American Art Therapy Association
1202 Allanson Rd.
Mundelein, IL 60060
arttherapy.org

American Association for Adult and Continuing Education
1200 Ninteenth St. NW
Washington, DC 20036
aaace.org

American Association of Colleges of Pharmacy
1426 Prince St.
Alexandria, VA 22314
aacp.org

American Association of Critical Care Nurses
Columbia Rd.
Aliso Viejo, CA 92656
aacn.org

American Association for Geriatric Psychiatry
7910 Woodmont Ave., Ste. 1050
Bethesda, MD 20814
aagpgpa.org

American Association of Health, Physical Education, Recreation,
    and Dance
1900 Association Dr.
Reston, VA 22091

American Association for Homecare
625 Slaters La.
Alexandria, VA 22314
aahomecare.org

American Association for Marriage and Family Therapy
1133 Fifteenth St. NW, Ste. 300
Washington, DC 20036
aamft.orgindex_nm.asp

American Bar Association
Commission on Legal Problems of the Elderly
1800 M St. NW
Washington, DC 20036
abanet.orgelderly/home.html

American Chiropractic Association
1701 Clarendon Blvd.
Arlington, VA 22209
amerchiro.org

American College of Health Care Administrators
1800 Diagonal Rd., #235
Alexandria, VA 22314
achca.org

American Counseling Association
5999 Stevenson Ave.
Alexandria, VA 22304
counseling.org

American Dance Therapy Association
2000 Century Plaza, Ste. 108
Columbia, MD 21044
adta.org

American Dental Association
211 E. Chicago Ave.
Chicago, IL 60611
ada.org

American Dietetic Association
216 W. Jackson Blvd.
Chicago, IL 60606
eatright.org

American Federation of Home Health Agencies
1320 Fenwick La., Ste. 100
Silver Spring, MD 20910

American Federation of State, County, and Municipal Employees
1625 L St. NW
Washington, DC 20036
wfse.org

American Health Care Association
1201 L St. NW
Washington, DC 20005
ahca.org

American Hospital Association
1 N. Franklin St.
Chicago, IL 60611
aha.org

American Institute of Architects
1735 New York Ave. NW
Washington, DC 20006
aia.org

American Licensed Practical Nurses Association
1090 Vermont Ave. NW, 1200
Washington, DC 20005

American Management Association
1601 Broadway
New York, NY 10019
amanet.org

American Medical Association
515 N. State St.
Chicago, IL 60610
ama-assn.org

American Medical Directors Association
10480 Little Patuxent Pkwy., Ste. 76B
Columbia, MD 21044
amda.com

American Music Therapy Association
8455 Colesville Rd., Ste. 100
Silver Spring, MD 20910
namt.com

American Nurses Association
600 Maryland Ave. SW, Ste. 100W
Washington, DC 20024
nursingworld.org

American Occupational Therapy Association, Inc.
1720 Montgomery La.
P.O. Box 31220
Bethesda, MD 20824
aota.org

American Optometric Association
243 N. Lindbergh Blvd.
St. Louis, MO 63141
aoanet.org

American Osteopathic Association
142 E. Ontario St.
Chicago, IL 60611
aoa-net.org

American Pharmaceutical Association
2215 Constitution Ave. NW
Washington, DC 20037
aphanet.org

American Physical Therapy Association
1111 N. Fairfax St.
Alexandria, VA 22314

American Psychiatric Association
1400 K St. NW
Washington, DC 20005
psych.org

American Psychological Association
Division of Adult Development and Aging
750 First St. NE
Washington, DC 20002
apa.org

American Society for Geriatric Dentistry
211 E. Chicago Ave.
Chicago, IL 60611

American Society of Group Psychotherapy and Psychodrama
301 N. Harrison St., Ste. 508
Princeton, NJ 08540
asgpp.org

American Society for Public Administration
1120 G St. NW
Washington, DC 20005
aspanet.org

American Speech-Language-Hearing Association
10801 Rockville Pike
Rockville, MD 20852
asha.org

Association for Adult Development and Aging
University of Arkansas
ELCF 137 Grad Ed
Fayetteville, AR 72701

Association for Educational Communications and Technology
1800 N. Stonelake Dr., Ste. 2
Bloomington, IN 47404
aect.org

Association of University Programs in Health Administration
730 Eleventh St. NW
Washington, DC 20001
aupha.org

Committee for Certification of Geriatric Pharmacy
1321 Duke St.
Alexandria, VA 22314

Health Occupation Students of America
c/o Rodrick Echols, President
Brown University
Mailbox # 5664
Providence, RI 02912
hosa.org

Home Health Services and Staffing Association
c/o Mara Brenner
1875 Eye St. NW
Washington, DC 20006

International Association of Counseling Services
101 S. Whiting St., Ste. 211
Alexandria, VA 22304

International Society for Retirement and Life Planning
1745 Jefferson Davis Hwy., 202
Arlington, VA 22202
isrplan.org

Joint Commission on the Accreditation of Healthcare Organizations
1 Renaissance Blvd.
Oakbrook Terrace, IL 60181
jcaho.org

Legal Services for the Elderly
130 W. Forty-second St., 17th Fl.
New York, NY 10036

Medical Group Management Association
104 Inverness Terrace E
Englewood, CO 80112
mgma.com

National Association of Activity Professionals
P.O. Box 5530
Sevierville, TN 37864
thenaap.com

National Association of Community Health Centers
1330 New Hampshire Ave. NW
Washington, DC 20036
nachc.com

National Association for Drama Therapy
733 Fifteenth St. NW, Ste. 330
Washington, DC 20005
nadt.org

National Association for Home Care
228 Seventh St. SE
Washington, DC 20003
nahc.org

National Association of Older Worker Employment Services
409 Third St. SW, Ste. 200
Washington, DC 20024

National Association for Poetry Therapy
5505 Connecticut Ave. NW, #280
Washington, DC 20015
poetrytherapy.org

National Association for Practical Nurse Education and Services
1400 Spring St., Ste. 310
Silver Spring, MD 20910

National Association of Professional Geriatric Care Managers
1604 N. Country Club Rd.
Tucson, AZ 85716
caremanager.org

National Association of Retired Federal Employees
N. Washington St.
Arlington, VA 22314
narfe.org

National Association of Senior Companion Project Directors
c/o Richard Tate
2195 Ironwood Ct.
Coeur d'Alene, ID 83814
nascpd.org

National Association of Social Workers
750 First Ave. NE
Washington, DC 20002
naswdc.org

National Association of State Directors of Vocational/Technical
    Education Consortium
444 N. Capitol St. NW, #830
Washington, DC 20001
infolit.orgmembers/nasdvte.htm

National Board of Certified Counselors
3-D Terrace Way
Greensboro, NC 27403
nbcc.org

National Certification Council for Activity Professionals
P.O. Box 62589
Virginia Beach, VA 23466
nccap.org

National Council for Therapeutic Recreation Certification
7 Elmwood Dr.
New City, NY 10956
nctrc.org

National Council for Therapy and Rehabilitation through
    Horticulture
9041 Comprint Court, Ste. 103
Gaithersburg, MD 20877

National Gerontological Nursing Association
7794 Grow Dr.
Pensacola, FL 32514
ngna.org

National League for Nursing
61 Broadway, 33rd Fl.
New York, NY 10019
nln.org

National Medical Association
1012 Tenth St. NW
Washington, DC 20001
nmanet.org

National Mental Health Association
1021 Prince St.
Alexandria, VA 22314
nmha.org

National Recreation and Park Association
22377 Belmont Ridge Rd.
Ashburn, VA 22003
nrpa.org

National Rehabilitation Association
633 S. Washington St.
Alexandria, VA 22314
nationalrehab.org

National Senior Service Corp. Directors Association
c/o Alan G. Lopatin
4958 Butterworth Pl. NW
Washington, DC 20016

National Staff Development Council
P.O. Box 240
Oxford, OH 45056
nsdc.org

National Student Nurses Association
555 W. Fifty-seventh St., #1327
New York, NY 10019
nsna.org

Opticians Association of America
7023 Little River Turnpike
Annandale, VA 22003

Professional Association of Health Care Office Management
461 E. Ten Mile Rd.
Pensacola, FL 32534
pahcom.com

Society of Geriatric Cardiology
Heart House
9111 Old Georgetown Rd.
Bethesda, MD 20814
sgcard.org

Society for Human Resource Management
1800 Duke St.
Alexandria, VA 22314
shrm.org

Visiting Nurse Associations of America
11 Beacon St., Ste. 910
Boston, MA 02108
vnaa.org

Appendix D

Organizations Serving Minority Elderly

Centro Gerontologico Latino
(Latino Gerontological Center)
120 Wall St., 23rd Fl.
New York, NY 10005
gerolatino.org

Hawaii-Pacific Gerontological Society
P.O. Box 3714
Honolulu, HI 968132
hpgs.org

National Asian Pacific Center on Aging
1511 Third Ave., Ste. 914
Seattle, WA 98101
napca.org

National Association for Hispanic Elderly
(Asociacion Nacional Pro Personas Mayores)
234 E. Colorado Blvd., Ste. 300
Pasadena, CA 90010

National Caucus and Center on the Black Aged
1220 L St. NW, Ste. 800
Washington, DC 20005
ncba-blackaged.org

National Hispanic Council on Aging
2713 Ontario Rd. NW
Washington, DC 20009
nhcoa.org

National Indian Council on Aging
10501 Montgomery Blvd. NE, Ste. 210
Albuquerque, NM 87110
nicoa.org

Native Elder Health Care Resource Center
University of Colorado Health Science Center
Campus Box AO11-13
4455 E. Twelfth Ave.
Denver, CO 80220
uchsc.edu/ai/nehcrc

Organization of Chinese Americans
1001 Connecticut Ave. NW, Ste. 601
Washington, DC 20036
ocanatl.org

Appendix E

Gerontology Periodicals

Activities, Adaptation and Aging
Haworth Press, Inc.
10 Alice St.
Binghamton, NY 13904

Adult Foster Care Journal
Human Sciences Press
233 Spring St.
New York, NY 10013

Age
American Aging Association
110 Chesley Dr.
Media, PA 19063

Age and Aging
British Geriatrics Society
Oxford University Press Inc.
2001 Evans Rd.
Cary, NC 27511

Aging
U.S. Administration on Aging
330 Independence Ave. SW
Washington, DC 20201

Aging and Cognition
University of Victoria
Dept. of Psychology
Victoria, BC
Canada V8W 3PS

Aging: Immunology and Infectious Disease
Maryann Liebert Inc. Publishers
12651 Third Ave.
New York, NY 10128

Aging Network News
P.O. Box 1223
McLean, VA 22 101

Aging News Alert
The Senior Services and Funding Report
CD Publications
8204 Fenton St.
Silver Spring, MD 20910

Aging Research and Training News
Business Publishers, Inc.
8737 Colesville Rd., Ste. 1100
Silver Spring, MD 20910

Aging and Society
The Journal of the Centre for Policy on Aging and
   the British Society of Gerontology
Cambridge University Press
40 W. Twentieth St.
New York, NY 10011

Alberta Council on Aging News
Alberta Council on Aging
501 10506 Jasper Ave.
Edmonton, AB
Canada T5J 2W9

American Journal of Geriatric Psychiatry
American Psychiatric Press, Inc.
1400 K St. NW
Washington, DC 20005

Behavior, Health and Aging
Springer Publishing Company
536 Broadway
New York, NY 10012

Canadian Journal on Aging
University of Guelph
MacKinnon Bldg.
Guelph, ON
Canada N1G 2W1

Centre on Aging News
Centre on Aging
University of Manitoba
Manitoba, Winnipeg
Canada R3T 2N2

Clinical Gerontologist
Haworth Press, Inc.
10 Alice St.
Binghamton, NY 13904

EAGLE: Exchange on Ageing, Law, and Ethics
Age Concern England
London, England SW16 4ER

Educational Gerontology
University of North Texas
1926 Chestnut St., No. 101
Denton, TX 76201

Educational Gerontology—An International Journal
Taylor and Francis Publishers
242 Cherry St.
Philadelphia, PA 19106

Elder Voices
National Indian Council on Aging
10501 Montgomery Blvd. NE, Ste. 210
Albuquerque, NM 87110

Experimental Gerontology
International Association of Gerontology
Pergamon Press
660 White Plains Rd.
Tarrytown, NY 10591

Focus on Geriatric Care and Rehabilitation
Aspen Publishers
200 Orchard Ridge Dr.
Gaithersburg, MD 20878

Frontiers in Aging Series
Human Sciences Press
233 Spring St.
New York, NY 10013

Generations United Magazine
Generations United
122 C St. NW, Ste. 820
Washington, DC 20001

Geriatric Nursing
Journal Subscription Service
11830 Westline Industrial Dr.
St. Louis, MO 63146

Geriatrics
Advanstar Communications Inc.
7500 Old Oak Blvd.
Cleveland, OH 44130

Gerontology and Geriatrics Education
Haworth Press, Inc.
10 Alice St.
Binghamton, NY 13904

Gray Panthers Network
Gray Panthers
733 Fifteenth St. NW, Ste. 437
Washington, DC 20006

Home Health Care Services Quarterly
Haworth Press, Inc.
10 Alice St.
Binghamton, NY 13904

The Hospice Journal
Haworth Press, Inc.
10 Alice St.
Binghamton, NY 13904

Human Resources and Aging Bulletin
Brookdale Center on Aging of Hunter College
1114 Avenue of the Americas, 40th Fl.
New York, NY 10036-7703

International Journal of Aging and Human Development
Baywood Publishing Company Inc.
26 Austin Ave.
Amityville, NY 11701

*International Journal of Experimental and
    Clinical Gerontology*
International Association of Gerontology
Publisher—S. Karger AG
26 W. Avon Rd.
P.O. Box 529
Farmington, CT 06085

International Journal of Technology and Aging
Human Sciences Press
233 Spring St.
New York, NY 10013

International Psychogeriatrics
Springer Publishing Company
536 Broadway
New York, NY 10012

Journal of Aging and Health
Sage Publications, Inc.
2455 Teller Rd.
Newbury Park, CA 91320

Journal of Aging and Judaism
Human Sciences Press
233 Spring St.
New York, NY 10013

Journal of Aging and Physical Activity
Human Kinetics Publishers Inc.
1607 N. Market St.
P.O. Box 5076
Champaign, IL 61825

Journal of Aging and Social Policy
Haworth Press, Inc.
10 Alice St.
Binghamton, NY 13904

Journal of Aging Studies
University of Florida
Dept. of Sociology
Gainesville, FL 32611

Journal of Applied Gerontology
Sage Publications, Inc.
2455 Teller Rd.
Newbury Park, CA 91320

Journal of Clinical and Experimental Gerontology
Marcel Dekker, Inc.
270 Madison Ave.
New York, NY 10016

Journal of Cross-Cultural Gerontology
Kluwer Academic Publishers
101 Philip Dr.
Norwell, MA 02061

Journal of Elder Abuse and Neglect
Haworth Press, Inc.
10 Alice St.
Binghamton, NY 13904

Journal of Geriatric Drug Therapy
Haworth Press, Inc.
10 Alice St.
Binghamton, NY 13904

Journal of Geriatric Psychiatry
64 Hancock Ave.
Newton Centre, MA 02159

Journal of Gerontological Nursing
Slack Inc.
6900 Grove Rd.
Thorofare, NJ 08086

Journal of Gerontological Social Work
Haworth Press, Inc.
10 Alice St.
Binghamton, NY 13904

Journal of Housing for the Elderly
Haworth Press, Inc.
10 Alice St.
Binghamton, NY 13904

Journal of Long Term Care Administration
Pride Foundation to Promote Real Independence for
   the Disabled and Elderly
391 Long Hills Rd.
P.O. Box 1293
Groton, CT 06340

Journal of Medical Humanities and Bioethics
Human Sciences Press
233 Spring St.
New York, NY 10013

Journal of Nutrition for the Elderly
Haworth Press, Inc.
10 Alice St.
Binghamton, NY 13904

Journal of Religious Gerontology
Haworth Press, Inc.
10 Alice St.
Binghamton, NY 13904

Journal of Women and Aging
Haworth Press, Inc.
10 Alice St.
Binghamton, NY 13904

Managing Senior Care
Business Publishers, Inc.
8737 Colesville Rd., Ste. 1100
Silver Spring, MD 20910

Nurseweek
1156-C Aster Ave.
Sunnyvale, CA 94086

Older Americans Report
Business Publishers, Inc.
8737 Colesville Rd., Ste. 1100
Silver Spring, MD 20910

Physical and Occupational Therapy in Geriatrics
Haworth Press, Inc.
10 Alice St.
Binghamton, NY 13904

Psychology and Aging
American Psychological Association
750 First St.
Washington, DC 20002

Research on Aging
Sage Publications, Inc.
2455 Teller Rd.
Newbury Park, CA 91320

Senior Care Professional
Community Development Services, Inc.
CD Publications
8204 Fenton St.
Silver Spring, MD 20910

Senior Citizen News
Alliance for Retired Americans
888 Sixteenth St. NW
Washington, DC 20006

Southwest Journal on Aging
Southwest Society on Aging
North Texas State University
P.O. Box 13346
Denton, TX 76203

Appendix F

Selected Readings

Achenbaum, W. Andrew. *Profiles in Gerontology: A Biographical Dictionary.* New York: Greenwood Publishing Group, 1995.

Baker, Mary Olsen, and Kathleen H. Wilber. "Educating Policy Gerontologists: The Impact of a Policy Specialization on Career Choice and Career Development." *Educational Gerontology* (April/May 1995) vol. 2, issue 3: 219–31.

Bureau of Labor Statistics. *Occupational Outlook Handbook.* Washington, DC: U.S. Government Printing Office, annual.

Chop, Walter, and Regula H. Robnett. *Gerontology for the Health Care Profession.* Philadelphia: Davis Company, 1999.

Everard, Kelly M., Pamela B. Teaster, and Elizabeth Dugan. "Surviving Your Graduate Gerontology Education and Entering the Job Market." *Educational Gerontology* (April/May 2000) vol. 26, issue 3: 285–300.

Farr, J. Michael, and LaVerne L. Ludden. *Best Jobs for the 21st Century.* Indianapolis, IN: JIST Works, Inc., 1999.

Gelford, Donald E. *The Aging Network: Programs and Services.* New York: Springer Publishing Co., 1999.

Giordano, Jeffrey A., Tom Rich, and Thomas A. Rich. *Gerontologist as an Administrator.* Westport, CT: Auburn House Publishers, 2001.

Gradler, Geoffrey C., and Kurt E. Schrammel. "The 1992–2005 Job Outlook in Brief," *Occupational Outlook Quarterly* (spring 1994), vol. 38, issue 1: 2–9.

Greenberg, Beverly. *Age Works—What Corporate America Must Do to Survive the Graying of America.* New York: Free Press, 2000.

Harkness, Helen. *Don't Stop the Career Clock: Rejecting the Myths of Aging for a New Way to Work in the 21st Century.* Palo Alto, CA: Davies-Black Publishers, 1999.

Hayes, David, ed. *Exploring Health Care Careers.* Chicago: Ferguson Publishing Co., 1998.

Hogstel, Mildred O. *Gerontology: Nursing Care of the Older Adult.* Albany, NY: Delmar Publishers, 2000.

Maddox, George L. *The Encyclopedia of Aging: A Comprehensive Resource in Gerontology and Geriatrics.* New York: Springer Publishing Co., 2001.

Mellor, M. Joanna, and Renee Solomon, eds. *Geriatric Social Work Education. Journal of Gerontological Social Work*, vol. 18, nos. 3 and 4: 218 pages.

Nathanson, Ilene L., and Tony T. Tirrito. *Gerontological Social Work: Theory into Practice.* Binghamton, NY: Haworth Press, 1998.

Neysmith, Sheila M., ed. *Critical Issues for Future Social Work Practice with Aging Persons.* New York: Columbia University Press, 1999.

Purcell, P. J. "Older Workers: Employment and Retirement Trends." *Monthly Labor Review* (Oct. 2000) vol. 123, no. 10: 19–30.

Robert, Roxanne, and Pearl M. Mosher-Ashley. "Factors Influencing College Students to Choose Careers Working with Elderly Persons." *Educational Gerontology* (Dec. 2000) vol. 26, no. 8: 725–36.

Safford, Florence, and George K. Krell, eds. *Gerontology for Health Professionals: A Practice Guide*, 2nd edition. Washington, DC: National Association of Social Workers, 1997.

Schneider, Robert L., Nancy P. Kropf, and Anne J. Kisor. *Gerontological Social Work: Knowledge, Service Settings and Special Populations*, 2nd edition. Belmont, CA: Wadsworth Press, 2000.

Taylor, Chris. "Cool Job Titles of the Millennium—Business Gerontologist." *BC Business*, vol. 27, issue 6: 14.

About the Author

ELLEN WILLIAMS is 4-H Agent for Rutgers Cooperative Extension of Monmouth County, New Jersey. In this role, she has promoted intergenerational programs linking youth and elders and has developed a training manual for teachers and youth services workers entitled *Intergenerational Programming—Linking Youth and Elders*. She is Vice President of Programs and Development for the New Jersey Intergenerational Network. She contributed to the report resulting in New Jersey legislation supporting grandparents' rights. Ms. Williams's oral history training was acknowledged as a significant factor in the success of the project "20th Century: An Oral History of Monmouth County."

Ms. Williams has had extensive experience in the gerontology field as a professor, administrator, consultant, program director, grants writer, speaker, and author. In academia, she has been the coordinator of the Gerontological Studies Program at Caldwell College in New Jersey and a faculty member in gerontology at New York University, Long Island University, and Kean College of New Jersey. She served as the director of a major multipurpose senior citizens center in Brooklyn and has been a program consultant to such groups as the New York City Parks Department Older Adult Unit and the Newark Teachers Union. Through funding from the Very Special Arts program of the Kennedy Center for the Performing Arts, she directed the Henry Fonda Senior Playwriting Program at the Actors Home, a retirement home for individuals having had careers in the performing arts.

Ms. Williams is co-author of the book *Recreation Programming and Leadership*. She graduated summa cum laude from the Leisure Services and Studies graduate program of Florida State University. For her present work as a 4-H Agent, she was awarded the Achievement in Service Award from the National Association of Extension 4-H Agents and the Diversity Award from Rutgers Cooperative Extension. As a Registered Drama Therapist, Ms. Williams has promoted intergenerational understanding by involving youth and elders in dramatizing situations that challenge ageism.